P9-EDY-053

The imaginative book of home decoration

Co
New concepts &

Po
D
I

W
Co

Dining

THE IMAGINATIVE BOOK OF HOME DECORATION

Author: Metamorphosis
Publishing director Nacho Asensio
Art director Carla Tábora
Texts Ana Ventura
Translation Harry Paul
Photography Melba Levick
Eugeni Pons/Piscinas Costa Brava
Pere Planells
Mihail Moldoveanu
Joan Mundó
Jordi Sarrà
Dominique Delaunay

David Cardelús
Francisco Po Egea
Relais Châteaux
Bill Timmerman
Peter Hyatt

Published in 2000
by Atrium International, s.a.

Ganduxer 115, 4º
Barcelona 08022 Spain
T. 34- 93 418 49 10
Fax 34- 93 211 81 39

e-mail: arcoedit@ibernet.com

ISBN:84-8185-225-2

DBL: B.11775-2000
Printed in Spain
Cayfosa - Quebecor
Sta Perpetua de Mogoda
(Barcelona)

Index

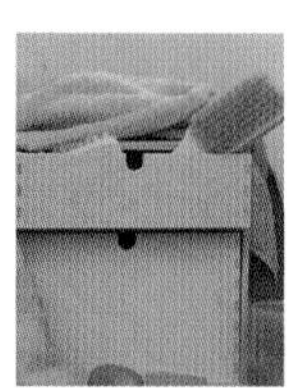
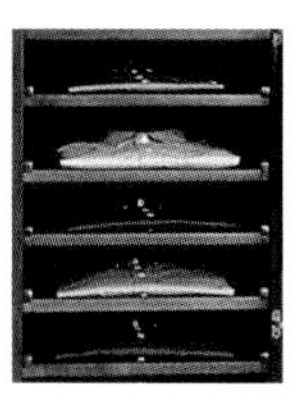

Introduction

“Sixteen brushstrokes of refined tastes”

When we are looking for ideas about decorating our home or simply want to be informed about what is happening in the world of decoration, we go to the bookshop searching for something original that will take us aback because of the way it deals with the subject.

“The imaginative book of home decoration” offers us a wide visual panorama of sixteen contemporary subjects which in their own right could be developed into an individual book.

In this book our aim has been to reveal little brushstrokes about each of the themes studied briefly. In the 176 pages we have set out to give the reader the opportunity to find out something about what today’s specialists in decoration are doing to make our homes more comfortable.

As always we tend towards practical solutions rather than spectacular projects which are only feasible with large budgets.

This book is a textbook of practical solutions affordable for any pocket. However, above all it is a selection of imaginative ideas put into practice by professionals in the relevant field.

In Metamorphosis we deal with everyday useful objects and spaces designed for living in. However, the credit must go to our colleagues with whom we have shared ideas and argued about tendencies.

Using our criteria of severe, positive critics, we have selected the projects successfully carried out which offer the reader the most ideas per square centimeter.

We admire and value the imagination the authors of the sixteen groups shown here, and therefore we are sure that they add up to make an impact on the reader who comes to this book, “The imaginative book of home decoration”, looking for effective ideas.

Metamorphosis

Conceiving the space

Space is our ally. It can be adapted to our needs making practical and cozy corners where we can read a book or quietly chat and enjoy being at home.

Dining & living rooms

Complements

und a table

living in colors

SANDEMAN
Maureen Duffy
DIE LADY IST FÜRS FEUER
Der Aufstand
Der verlorene Stand

The way the furniture is laid out can help to define zones within the space.

Conceiving the space

Balanced and coming together. Understanding the space and the elements in it is the first step to good decoration. The orientation, the light coming through the windows, and the views are external factors which should be born in mind. The objective assessment of the space and its possibilities is a key step towards getting the decoration program right. Each space is distinct, has it own characteristics, and therefore requires special treatment.

The colors and materials of the ceilings and walls become very important. The materials chosen for each space must be compatible with the aesthetics and the practical needs.

The furniture can be moved around to give form to the space and to define the style. We can create gathering zones, separate off different ambiences and play off mass against emptiness. The furniture is a basic decoration recourse which we can put to work for us.

The overall effect created by all these elements -materials, color, lighting and furniture- is fundamental to decide the style and ambience of the space we are decorating. There must be a general, balanced idea behind all the project so that the style is unified and coherent. A good concept of space and correct element distribution are fundamental to make the space practical and comfortable.

Introducing elements with a strong compositional character orders the space.

Natural illumination powerfully reinforces the perception that the room is one space.

Complements

Flexible and multifunctional. The dining room and the living room are spaces where many different activities take place so they have to adapt to various situations and needs. This created the necessity for easily movable furniture, suitable for different uses and without a fixed role in the space.

These elements are most important in the living room. Examples of furniture which can seem unimportant but which help us to do the daily activities in comfort are small tables, on which to leave a book, a drinks cabinet, or a pouffe on which to rest your feet.

Some complementary furniture is designed for different functions.

The usefulness of this type of furniture is as important as the aesthetics. Of course, they must be in the same style as the general ambience unless you very carefully use them to introduce a specific touch of originality to break the monotony. As always, organizing the space rationally and with flexibility is important to make the space work, so do not over fill it with complementary elements.

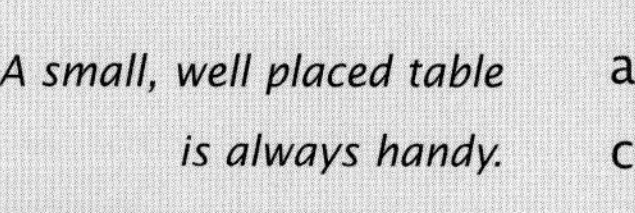

A small, well placed table is always handy.

The prime role of the space is as a coming together area so the furniture must invite people to sit down and to chat, something which relies heavily on the sofas and armchairs. The latter are especially crucial because of their size. Carpets or rugs can mark out a zone and the furniture can then be distributed around it. A central element, like a chimney or a table, helps to arrange the space.

Combining different accessory furniture will help us to create a flexible space.

Afterwards the complementary furniture comes into the picture, being arranged in such a way as to make the space flexible. Heavy furniture in a small space would reduce the sensation of freedom. The furniture layout plays a key role in the ambience of the space.

Around a table

Organized and functional. Sitting around a table to enjoy the food in company of others is almost a ritual.

A table and some chairs are sufficient to create an eating area.

We can fall back on formulas which break with the idea of a traditional dining room.

The dining room has a composition that permits few variations. Inevitably the table is center stage and dictates the way the rest of the space is organized. Rarely does another piece of furniture overshadow the table, although, sometimes a sideboard can do so. The chairs around the table reinforce its protagonism and organizational role. If we have abundant space, we can break away from this traditional formula and spread the chairs around the dining room, or even around other rooms. This will give the table a different role, almost like a sculpture, especially appropriate when the table has a secondary role because it is only used on special occasions and therefore does not have to offer its classic image with the chairs around it.

The furniture used to store the plates, cutlery and tablecloths is the second essential element. Placing them in cupboards near the table will give a rational space. A less traditional solution is to apply minimalism principles and to hide the objects away in cupboards built into the wall, or in furniture which does not match the classic image of dining room furniture.

Nowadays the most common formula is a dining and living room in one, although it may not adapt to our needs. Separating them can be a problem if space is limited. However, the situation can be improved by using furniture to divide the space instead of walls, which tend to take away light and further reduce small spaces.

The options are infinite and go from the classic folding screen or sideboard through to a bookcase. We could even try out more daring solutions like a low

The details both compositional and decorative, play a major role.

A sofa with daring lines and colors gives a touch of originality to the space.

wall, curtains or a glass partition. Anything is valid if it is better suited to our necessities.

Living in color

Elegant and cozy.

Living rooms and dining rooms, where we spend a great deal of our leisure time, are rooms for receiving people and for social life, meaning that the decoration is highly important. The furniture, the illumination, the colors and the details must all be carefully controlled. The illumination requires a lot of attention because a room with well chosen and matched colors and furniture can be spoiled if the lighting is sloppy or incongruent. Good lighting is nothing more and nothing less than getting the intensity right in every space bearing in mind the activities carried out. In the dining room the lighting must favor the table, without sacrificing practical considerations. One or two overhead lamps may not be enough. Ambiental lighting is useful for giving unity to the project, and at the same time it makes up for any lack of light. Lamps stands or table lamps can focus light on specific areas and will therefore help to make the space appear smaller, it this is the effect desired. If they are carefully placed, neither blinding nor producing unwanted shadows, they can round off practical and effectual lighting. Another key factor is the color for it can modify the style and character of an ambience. Getting the color right can mean getting it all right. Color must go hand in hand with the image projected. Dark tones like olive green or burgundy red give the space a solemn look and

Bold and amusing compositions go down well in a living room.

Color is capable of modifying a space and giving it great warmth.

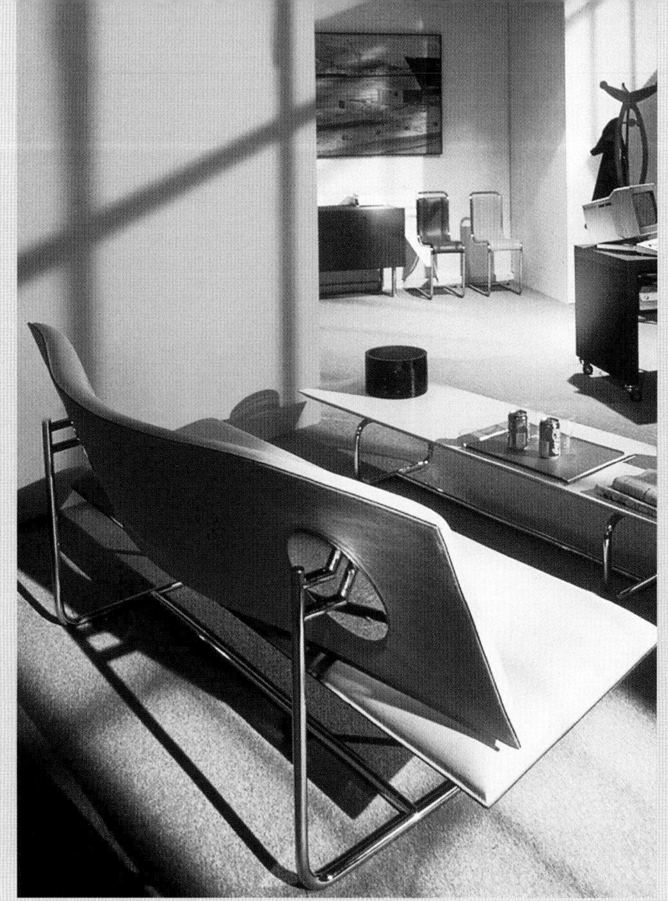

Yellow is a cheerful and energetic color that goes well with modern furniture.

combine well with golds and yellows to produce an elegant, luxurious effect. Dark blue tones are just as elegant, although somewhat less formal.

Living in colors

Playing with the colors can produce surprisingly attractive results.
Yellows make the rooms more summery because of their energy and luminosity. The classic options, whites and the neutral beige tones, give the space a solemn, timeless feel. However, combined with other tones they can produce intimate and hospitable ambiences. Just as in other parts of the house, little details can influence decisively. Candles on a table, a bunch of fresh flowers, the way the curtains are held or cushions on the sofa are just some examples of details which reveal to the visitor that we are discerning when caring for our home. It is worth considering what candles can do. Their glowing, flickering light is unmatchable by any artificial illumination and therefore the atmosphere conjured up is unique. We should let their seductive, enchanting power come into play not only on special occasions but more often. Some moments in our lives or some events deserve a special effort. Anniversaries and celebrations are the perfect time for enjoying all the pleasures of the decoration. The Christmas meals or summer garden parties are a good enough justification for devoting attention to the table and calling on all the decoration recourses. Everything, candles, fresh or dry flowers, colors and complements can be used to express our creative table decorating ideas. Special occasions offer us the opportunity to enjoy the results of our decorating.

Playing with colors offers surprising and atractive results

Little details like candles and flowers are essential to the atmosphere.

The right sofa

Chairs, chairs, chairs

Designing a bed

Home furniture adorns our house, stores objects and allows us to rest comfortably. Furniture is our most faithful ally for transforming empty spaces into inhabitable rooms.

Home furniture

Essential and practical

bookcases

The right sofa

The right sofa

Comfortable and cozy. Sofas have become the most important part of the new living rooms. Their size, robustness and weight almost anchor them to their spot, firmly marking out the limit and defining an area. They can be arranged around a table, a rug or sometimes around a chimney or TV. The layout is not random for it creates a friendly atmosphere for get-togethers in which we feel comfortable sitting down and chatting. However, these types of spaces need flexibility, which in fact is restricted by the sofas and so often we intermingle armchairs, pouffes or even normal chairs, moving them about to suit our needs. Choosing a sofa is not an easy task.

A Charles sofa.

It has elegant lines, optimum for a modern living room.

A distinctive sofa greatly helps to define the ambience.

Neutral tone tapestries are elegant and always in fashion.

Sofas have special power to create and define spaces.

Not only must the sofa fit in with the ambience and the style of the space, it must also be comfortable and practical. Analyzing its use will help us to choose. If animals or children live in the house, it is best to avoid light tapestries. Old people have problems getting up from low models. Aesthetics are also important. In the market we can find a multitude of models, from classic wood structures and bold patterns through to minimalist, straight lined modern ones. At least one of them will fit our needs. Alternatively you can resort to a specialist shop which makes them to measure or restores and reupholsters old sofas.

The right sofa

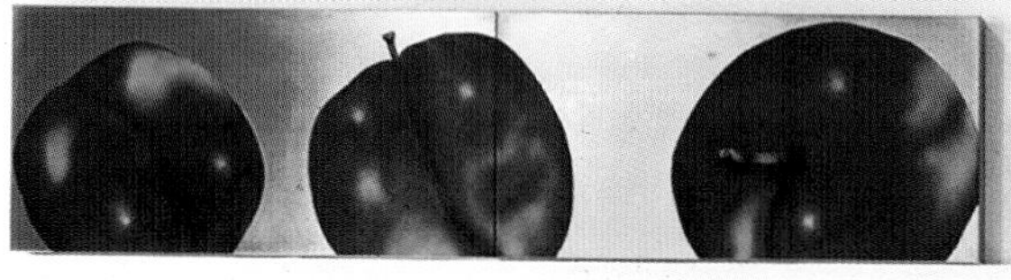

The suggestive and imaginative forms of a sofa create a homely ambience.

Some pieces of furniture, among them sofas, are excellent for introducing dashes of color.

Deco chair with arms.

Party chair.

Only you chair.

Dorsus chair.

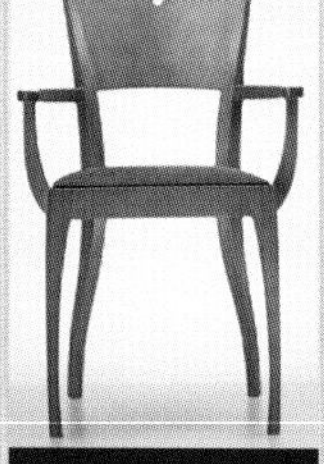

Arabesco chair.

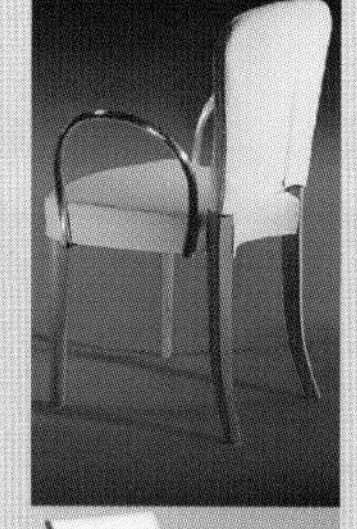

Margot chair.

Barbara chair.

Barbara chair with arms.

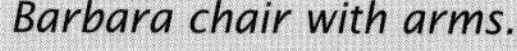

Apta chair.

Chairs, chairs, chairs

Versatile and practical. Chairs, so necessary for a whole range of activities, can fit into any corner. They are among the most used furniture in the home. They come in a variety of materials and finishings, for example, wood, steel and wrought metal, with or without upholstery. The rule about choosing with practical criteria as well as for looks still applies. Sturdy and resistant materials should be chosen for the kitchen or for a dining room where the chairs are going to come in for heavy use. In these cases, upholstery is not recommendable although we could protect them with a cover or choose a material that stands up to the dirt. This will help us to keep them in good shape.

In the living room or dining room we could opt for a more delicate yet resistant model. The upholstery can be played off against the tapestry of the sofa and the curtains, and is ideal for bringing in color and animating the space.

Chairs are also needed in offices, studies and libraries. In these spaces we work and so may have to spend long hours. Comfort is at a premium. The most suitable ones are chairs with little wheels and height and back angle adjustment facilities. They have the advantage of being adaptable to the height of the table.

It is quite difficult to calculate the quantity of chairs that a house may need. Perhaps it would appear logical that a family of six could get by with eight chairs, but it does not work like that. When friends or relatives come to dinner or supper there can easily be ten to twelve people and so we will have to borrow chairs from other rooms. If we do not have enough space to store the chairs, we can use foldable ones.

Getting a beautiful design that looks effortlessly put together is clearly an aim.They are normally quite cheap and four or five should be sufficient for any situation.

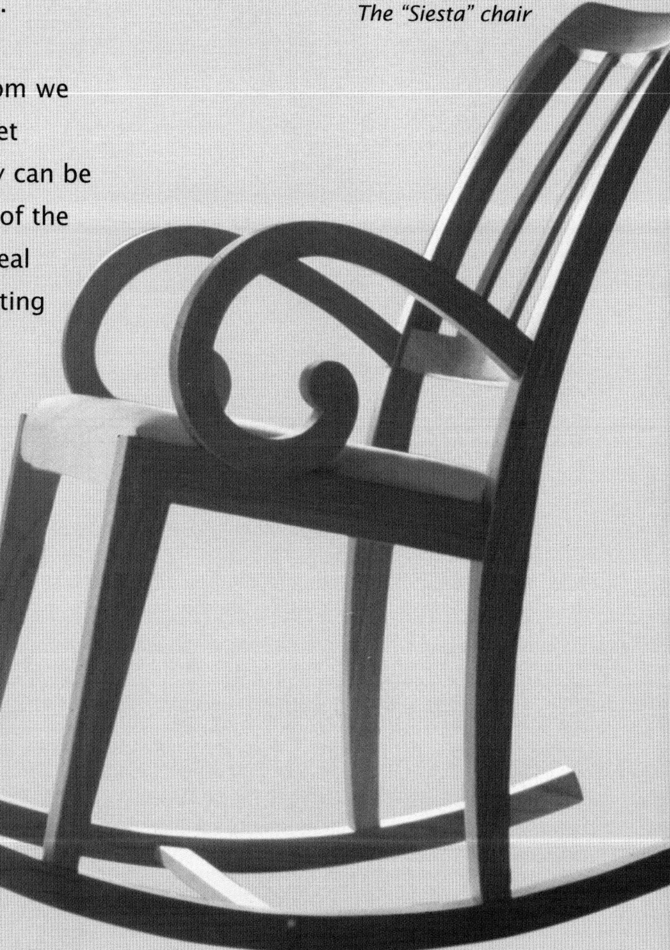

The "Siesta" chair

rs

ra 1 chair.

letta chair with arms.

letta chair.

orm chair.

Maya chair.

sina chair.

Tross chair.

rina chair.

gora chair.

High quality furniture is created when the design goes right down to the smallest details.

Designing a bed

Snug and intimate.

The bed is so important not only because it helps to determine the aesthetics of the room, but also because it is vital for getting a good night's sleep and feeling refreshed in the morning.

Its structure, hidden away below the blankets, determines how comfortable we are, something as important as its aspect. A professional salesman should inform us which bed best suits our age and physical constitution.

Beds influence the ambience of the bedroom, regardless of whether they are big, small, high, low, old or modern. The headboard and the feet can be made of different materials, wood, wrought metal, or steel, and can come in distinct forms. In the design plan the bed linen should not be forgotten because the sheets, pillow cases, eider downs and duvets can be powerful decorative elements and an ideal complement to round off an overall effect. The necessities of modern life have meant that new types of multi-functional beds have come into existence and which are better adapted to our needs. Nest beds, with a storage space or another bed underneath, are ideal for guest bed-rooms or small rooms . Couches are ever practical, allowing us to store clothes and objects beneath them. Other models incorporate shelves that are useful as bedside tables. Blankets and pillows can be stored in practical drawers or compartments.

The bed is a key element for defining the style of the bedroom.

Essential and practical bookcases

Essential and practical bookcases

Design can produce stunningly beautiful details.

Order and composition. Book cases and shelving are imperative in studies, libraries, offices, and even sometimes in the living room. Storing and classifying books, compacts, documents and photographs requires a rationalized and simple system so that we take up as little space as possible. What is needed on a daily basis must be separated from the material used only occasionally. The latter can be kept in more out of the way places, like high up cupboards or attics. Books and compacts are easy to order and give a pleasing aspect when neatly shelved, adding color and texture to the space. Documents and photos have to be placed in boxes or files before being placed on the shelves, practical fittings which besides storing many things also contribute to the aesthetics. A TV or music system will liven up the more staid look of the books. The lighting is important to get the aesthetics right and to allow you to view the books. Ceiling illumination tends to throw shadows on to the spines, although it can be attractive. A few lamp-stands or spotlights can solve this problem. A third alternative is to have lighting incorporated into the shelving itself. One possible variation is to have little cupboard compartments on the shelves.

Practical furniture fills the spaces around our home.

One option is to integrate the furniture into the architecture.

Books become a decorative element.

The right furniture will give us an ordered, friendly space.

Light & space

peaceful atmosphere

Decoration gets into the most personal part of the home. The bedroom is the place which reveals most about our personality while making us feel safe and comfortable.

Bedrooms & children's bedrooms

Getting the most out

ildren's bedrooms

The curtains allow us to control the daylight.

Light and space

Secluded and intimate. The bedroom is the most personal space in the home and therefore our identity is reflected in all the decoration details. Our most personal objects are here making it the space where we feel secure and comfortable, surrounded by what we value and means a lot to us. These factors add up to give even more prominence to the decoration. Despite the misleading first impression, the decoration of the room where we repose is vital. We fall asleep with the sensations emitted by the ambience and the decoration, and the first thing we perceive on waking up is the feel of the bedroom as it influences our moods.

Natural illumination brings life to all spaces and has a tremendous feel-good factor.

It is crucial that the bedroom has an external window so that we are aware of the passage of time and of the weather. Moreover, the air most be able to circulate to avoid stuffiness. Daylight streaming through the windows converts rooms into places where we want to be, either reading a book on the bed or in an armchair, watching TV, or simply taking it easy. The bed is the most important element in the room. It ensures that we wake up invigorated in the morning and it visually dominates the room. Its size and style are critical in ensuring a unified and balanced ambience. Secondary zones can be developed for other activities like reading or even studying. A couple of armchairs and a table can be used to set up a little, but very useful, work area.

Let some sunshine into your bedroom. A cheerful mood helps you to relax

The bed is the center of attention in the bedroom so be careful with its aesthetics.

A peaceful atmosphere

Intimate and upbeat. The bedroom must transmit sensations of security and optimism, making us feel at ease in it. All of the elements that make up the decoration are important to this end, right from the large colored surfaces down to the smallest details.

A peaceful atmosphere

Arranging the space is the first step. It is tricky to place the bed in the exactly right spot although we can follow general guidelines like placing it near the window so that it dominates most of the space. Popular tradition affirms that when lying on a bed our feet should be pointed northward. The oriental science Feng shui offers basic principles for placing not only beds but all sorts of furniture The materials too play a role in the whole look and feel. Heat retaining flooring, like carpets or parquet, are pleasant not only because of their warmth but also because of their softness on our bare feet. On the walls, matte paint finishes or wallpaper look good. Be careful to choose natural products.

The style of the bed must match the rest of the room to create a unified project.

Wood is especially suitable for a bedroom. Its aspect and feel when touched are warm, and it is not a hard material. If we decide on steel or metal furniture, bear in mind that they are cold and hard so do not overdo the effect. Try to combine them with more affable materials. Even though we sleep in the bedroom, the lighting is very important. Here we dress, read, watch TV and listen to music. Some

Sheets, curtainsand fabrics add spice and feel to the ambience.

Being careful in the way the cushions are placed reveals our commitment to tasteful decoration.

A peaceful atmosphere

Complementary furniture makes the room comfortable and functional.

of these activities require special lighting. Plain overhead lighting will not be suitable because when lying on the bed it can get in our eyes.

Lampshades, table lamps or wall lights can offer us illumination adaptable to the different situations. Fabrics are especially important in the bedroom because the sheets, cushions, pillows and curtains animate the room. The colors and the patterns must be easy to combine so that we can introduce small changes without undoing the whole effect. A blanket on the bed or on an armchair, and the way we arrange the pillows, curtains, or the mosquito net are all little details that can give a final touch of style to the space.

Getting the most out of the space

Practical and functional. Modern bedroom furniture has been devised using ideas carefully thought out to take advantage of the space available. Frequently modern residences have small rooms in which distinct activities are carried out.

Something of our personality and approach to life comes across through the little details.

Getting the most out of

Imaginative space saving gives classy solutions.

The furniture enables us to create practical, fun compositions.

The bedroom is one room in the house where a great deal of space is used for keeping clothes, books and other objects. Built in cupboards are a practical solution, but sometimes not enough.

Available in the market we can find beds adaptable to any situation. Bunk beds are classic but they are not always very practical. Other models include beds at different levels and at the same time offer drawers and useful storage facilities for clothes and other things. Foldable beds on wheels are ideal for guest rooms or children's bedrooms.

As studying or working in the bedroom has caught on, original and practical table inventions have appeared on the market. Some can be folded away and stored under the bed or in the cupboard.
All these solutions may seem practical and even diverting but we have to analyze objectively to what extent they are going to meet our needs. A foldable table or chair is commonsense if it is only used on occasions, but it can become bothersome if we need it every day.
Maybe moving the study or work area to another room will be more rational in the long run.

Children's bedrooms

Colorful and fun. Children's bedrooms deserve special attention because children's needs are different to an adult's. It is not necessary to follow the traditional formula of a baby's room. A child's space must be designed thinking about their needs. Safety comes before decoration both in the materials used, as well as the paints and varnishes. Also the furniture must not have hard nor sharp edges and it must be of a size which the children can live with. However, this does not mean we have to resort to miniature furniture which would be obsolete after a couple of years. A table and a few low

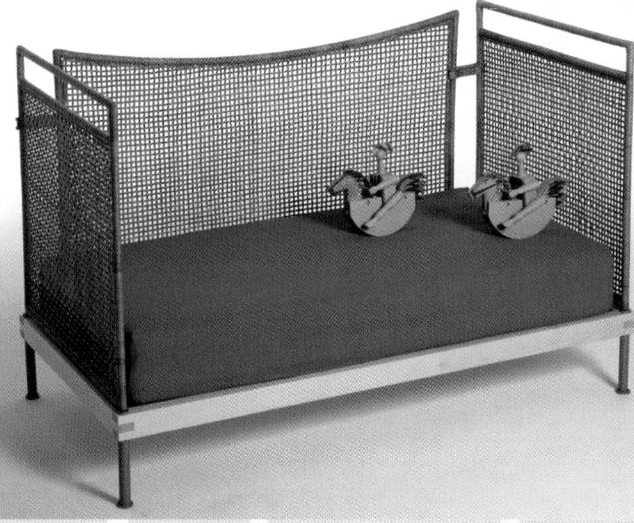

Furniture especially designed for children is lively and fun.

Children's bedrooms

chairs are sufficient for the child to have a space where to play and where he or she feels comfortable. Adaptability is crucial for these spaces because children grow rapidly, and their needs and tastes change just as quickly. Alterations will have to be introduced without breaking the budget. Fabrics, curtains, rugs, bed linen, and the color of the walls and furniture can all help to renovate the space.

A funky cupboard will make the children's bedroom less formal.

Color influences our mood which explains why color decoration has come into fashion for children's rooms. Different tones stimulate in distinct ways: yellow and red are lively and energetic. Green and blue help to wind down and relax. Children have their own tastes and beliefs and taking decisions about their own private space will help them in their development. Nobody can decide better than them what their space should be like so that they feel at home.

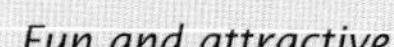

Fun and attractive.

Practical and functional compositions are optimal for children's bedrooms.

Daylight

Fabrics, carpets, flower

curtains

Lamps, flowers, candles, curtains, carpets. These are some of the small details that make a difference and give a personal characteristic touch to the decoration.

Decorative elements

Small details, great solu

Little details are imperative to unify the styles and get a coherent overall look.

Daylight

Changing and captivating. Natural light has a power and a pureness unmatchable by artificial lighting. The light that flows in through windows, balconies, skylights and fanlights illuminates the surfaces, constantly changing during the day.

It would be an error to plan the artificial illumination of a space without taking into consideration the daylight. The morning sunshine makes the colors brighter and snappier. The afternoon radiance favors relaxed tones, and the evening light brings calm, dark shades. When night falls, artificial lighting comes into play.

Here the lighting creates an atmosphere perfect for relaxing.

Natural illumination has the capacity to make a residence comfortable and soothing. It allows us to see the passing of the day, enjoying the alluring tones that the space acquires under its beams. Natural daylight is so pure and intense that working in it is easy on the eyes. Consequently it is logical to place desks or work tops near the windows. The opposite problem is if there is too much light: windows, blinds, shutters and curtains are fundamental for controlling the amount of light that gets in, rather like a lampshade. They filter the light and spread it uniformly around the space, being indispensable for rooms which receive direct sunlight.

Light influences the colors, but the colors also feed back on to the light. A color changes in tone during the day depending on the light cast on it. The amount of light the color reflects back depends on its clarity or darkness.

It is beyond doubt that light exercises a considerable influence on the decoration and has to be controlled if we are to achieve the desired ambience.

Daylight is a prevailing consideration for getting the most out of the decoration.

The light from a lamp or the way the table is laid are highly decorative details.

Fabrics, carpets, flowers and curtains

Style and good taste. Some decoration complements are vital for finishing a good project design. The way the space is handled and the furniture arrangement are important steps but the decoration program does not end here. Just as a person puts on clothes everyday, a space, too, needs to be dressed. Carpets, curtains, fabrics, wall hangings and flowers offer us the textures and colors to do this. Although curtains are important for aesthetics, without them the windows would be cold, they also have a practical use: our home must cut us off and isolate us from the outside world. Curtains filter the light and keep prying eyes out. As for aesthetics, curtains can add a touch of class with their fabrics, patterns, colors and the way they are hung. There are many varieties: net curtains, lace curtains, venetian curtains, drapes, rolling ones. We are sure to find some which match our needs and tastes.

The double function of carpets is to make the space warmer and more comfortable with their softness, above all when we are walking barefoot and the flooring is too hard or cold. Moreover, some carpets are so decorative that they can be considered works of art. Their elegance, attractive colors and patterns enhance the floor, often drawing a decoration project together. Carpets can also divide the space, creating sub-zones around which the furniture is organized. If a living room seems rather dull or unwelcoming, a carpet can focus the project and liven it up. Flowers are the classic way of animating a space. Their colors, fragrance and the way they seem to celebrate being part of nature probably cannot be equaled by any other decoration object. How they are arranged, and the vase, must also fit in with the ambience.

The way we fold away the curtains or arrange flowers gives an idea of our taste for details.

Small details, great solutions

Spot on and funny. The way objects are laid on a table, some candlesticks, tucking away the curtains or hanging some paintings, all of these are basic details which help to create quality and stylish designs. A whole host of objects can be used as highly decorative twists, some of them rely on beauty, others

In this living room we can appreciate how every detail has been taken care of to liven up the room.

Small details can have a great influence on the decoration.

on curiosity, and still others on their color scheme. However, whatever lies behind them, the objective is always the same: to make the decoration stand out for its creativity.

Small details are not only the objects we add in with the decoration. They can be structural or the way the space is divided up. For example, a stretch of wall beautifully tiled can be a structural detail strong enough to organize all the decorative program and to be the center of attention.

Curtains or a blanket on a sofa give style and ambience.

Details can be expressed through materials as well as objects, and the form in which the latter are arranged.

Other details can be ephemeral and change with the seasons or the festivities. Little details can take some colors or textures from outside and bring them into our home. Bright spring or summer flowers or a few logs of wood by the fire in winter are little things that produce a welcoming effect. This is even more important in areas where we receive people, the living room, the dining room or the hall, because they tell the visitor something about us. Sometimes people want their homes to say something personal. The hall is the first space we see in the home and first impressions count for a lot. Therefore make the decoration effectual, with a hint of theater, and stylish. Some flowers, a hat on a stand, or an umbrella will all add points of interest. Even though other areas of the house may be essentially practical, like the kitchen or the bathroom, the little singularities are still important. A fruit bowl or ceramic plates in the food area add a note of color. In the bathroom, richly textured towels or fragrant soaps will subtly embellish the ambience.

In this living room every detail has been placed carefully to create a fresh atmosphere.

Conserving food

The food handling area

Preparing the food is a pleasure in spaces where the outstanding functionality has been combined with aesthetic and structural perfection. This is the challenge for modern kitchen designers.

Kitchen

Time to cook

Storage

Cupboards which allow us to see what is inside are decorative elements.

Conserving food

Neat and practical. A multitude of objects are stored in the kitchen, food, saucepans and tablecloths are just a few examples. If the kitchen is going to be an efficient and workable space they will have to be ordered and arranged tidily and conveniently. However, preserving food requires more than order: the temperature and humidity must be right, and the food often has to be isolated. The classic concept of a larder or pantry, today somewhat dated, was based on finding a suitable, fresh, dry, isolated and dark place where to store food.

Keeping the kitchen neat and tidy with a place for everything will ensure that it is functional.

Normally the kitchen is a little warmer than the rest of the home due to the oven. The larder should be away from any direct heat source, even, ironically, the fridge. Of course cleaning or other chemical materials could also be hazardous, so keep them away too. Fresh produce, fruit and vegetables ought not to be stored in the kitchen where the higher temperatures would make them go off more quickly. A terrace by the kitchen is a great solution but if, unfortunately, this is not the case the best idea is to place them in a refrigerator with a specially designed compartment. Drinks, fruit juices through to wine, present us with a similar quandary. A room with cellar-like conditions is the best bet, or as an alternative a fridge for the juices and a cool place for the wine.

Here the furniture allows the utensils to be seen.

The kitchen too is a space for perfect aesthetics and decoration.

The food handling area

Functional and imaginative. The kitchen is surely the area of the house where the practical aspect is most important. Aesthetics come after but must not be forgotten. Our first objective must be to make the kitchen functional, a concept which can be divided into three necessities: safety, efficiency and avoiding unnecessary movements. To achieve these ends, careful planning is called for. When we know how much space we have available we must draw an imaginary triangle the corners of which will be for the three basic kitchen zones: storage, preparation and cooking. Our most frequent comings and goings will be along the outline of the triangle. The traditional U or L shaped kitchens are, in fact, the practical application of this principle. Doors, furniture or any other potential obstacles should not be allowed to get in our way, and the cooking area must not be too far from the preparation zone because it is dangerous to carry hot pans around. Avoid this as much as is possible.

When we have the right balance between these different areas, we can dedicate individual attention to each one. Foremost is the preparation area because that is where we will spend most time. Our objective is to design a space that enables us to work comfortably. The sink is the key element so, logically, in the market there are a multitude of different models on sale, among which we can find one that suits our needs. A special work top

Preparing and cooking the food requires separate but related zones.

There is no reason why anybody's kitchen should be less than beautiful.

The cooking zone comes into its own. It need not be hidden away.

surface is necessary, strong enough to resist water, little knife cuts and high temperatures. The illumination should be plentiful and direct. Although we have focused on being practical, in decoration the looks are always important. A functional area is quite uninviting if it is not comely and stylish. The colors, materials, textures and details are little features that will mean we are only too happy to spend some time in the kitchen.

Time to cook

Tradition and design.

The cooking area of a kitchen attracts a lot of attention. Back in the old times the fire was the center of social activity in the homes, or caves. The dwellings were organized around them.

Today cooking elements are as much about technology as they are about design. They must be pleasing to look at as well as practical. The kitchen rings, both gas and electricity, are no longer staid, off-putting objects. Today they can be integrated into the kitchen design project. Pure contemporary kitchens are often reliant on stainless steel, which has been a great success, both for its looks and for its practicality. Cooking hoods no longer have to be hidden away by other furniture; they have become design elements worthy of being admired. The introduction of new materials like heat-resistant glass and wood, made possible by technological advances, has spawned revolutionary formulas in the kitchen. Now many options are available, from the traditional kitchen with a large, prominent cooking area, through to kitchens based

The most modern design tendencies have reached the kitchen offering innovative results.

The influence of industrial kitchens is visible in the cooking zone.

A wooden doored cupboard permits us to store a wide diversity of objects.

on pure, pristine lines and a subtle, minimalist cooking hood. We can find all sorts of styles which mean that attractiveness does not have to be sacrificed for practicality. The aesthetics of the kitchen need not be out of tune with the rest of the residence.

Storage

Spot on and efficient. Things inevitably have to be stored in the kitchen. Crockery, cutlery, tablecloths and a whole variety of objects for cleaning need to be put away neatly. Dividing the space up into zones according to functions can aid us. Crockery and tablecloths should be stored near the dining room, cleaning products near the terrace and away from the food. Some basic guidelines have to be established so that space is defined in a practical manner. The objects, too, can be classified according to their use. Some glassware and cutlery are only used on special occasions and can therefore be kept in the dining room, or even the living room. Objects used daily should be kept at hand and readily available.

Built-in closets with sliding doors mean we can get the most out of the space.

Do not forget about the 'work triangle'. Knives, spoons, plates and all sorts of pots are necessary to prepare the food. A waste disposal unit is another must. The pots, casserole dishes and other utensils have to be kept near the cooking zone. All this means that the kitchen is like a laboratory where order and a good system are necessary to work quickly and efficiently. To help us to run it smoothly we must have a clear program, dividing the zones up logically according to their functions, and then we will be able to work without interruptions.

Attractive and eye-catching. Cupboards and shelves are the basics of storage. One option is to play down their presence by blending them in stylistically with the kitchen decoration. Alternatively, they can be independent elements that stand out for their singularity and individual style. It is up to us.

If we have gone for a traditional kitchen, in which the other essential elements have their own character, the option of emphasizing the individuality of the storage elements has a lot in its favor. A cupboard with crystal doors, either translucent or transparent, can be imaginative and allows us to see what is inside. High quality crockery or bowls can be displayed on a shelf as part of a neat, well looked after storage system. However, if we choose a modern kitchen, steering clear of the topics, it would be better to go for low key cupboards. Sliding or folding doors hide away the objects, rendering it less necessary to store them so neatly. If there is a small eating zone, we could install some shelves or cupboards and thus give this area a degree of independence. A table on its own seems quite insignificant, but combined with a sideboard or cupboard it will inevitably resemble a dining room. Decoration objects and subtle ornaments will fit in nicely.

Translucent glass offers us an attractive image of the objects stored inside the cupboard.

unctional & efficient

Tables & chair

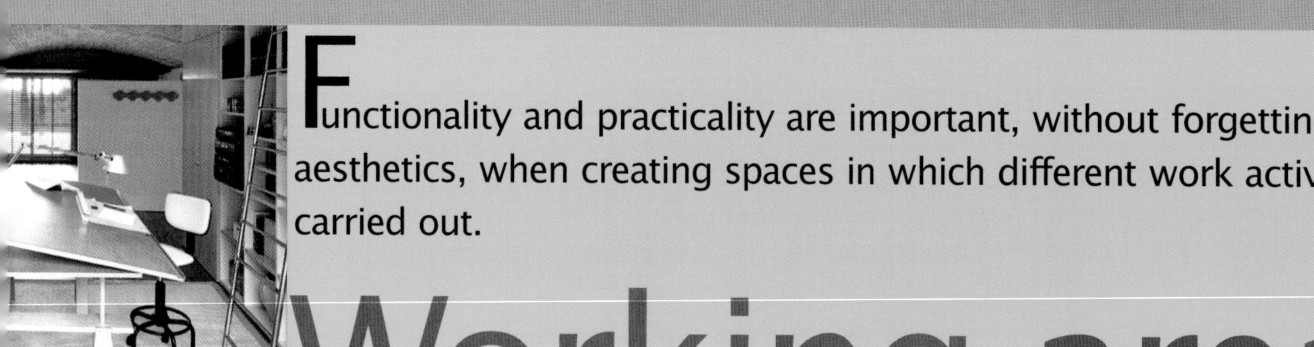

Functionality and practicality are important, without forgetting about aesthetics, when creating spaces in which different work activities will be carried out.

Working areas

pecial places

rganizing furniture

Functional and efficient

Studies and libraries must be functional spaces.

Let yourself concentrate: the home must not take over the office.

Attractive and ingenious. The home is not just a place where we while away our leisure time. Work zones have become increasingly necessary: aesthetics and practicality have been forced to come up with common solutions. These spaces must have certain elements in every case: a table, chairs and adequate work lighting. The quid of the question is to lay out the furniture so that it is easy to use. First of all examine the space rationally, dividing it into classified zones: work, storage, filing, etc, according to our needs. Then join the zones together with an efficient systematic approach. Comfort when working is at a premium. Everything we may need must be handy so that we can concentrate on the task and thus increase our productivity or inspiration.

Today it is impossible to work without a computer and therefore our table must allow one to be installed comfortably. Lighting which avoids eye strain is another important factor. Normally the work table should be near the window, and if we are right handed it is better for the light to come from the left side, there by ruling out annoying shadows. Basking in daylight and enjoying privileged views will certainly raise our spirits and relax us, above all if the work is stressful. However, when the sun goes down we will need to have adequate artificial lighting. Shadows from lamps could be bothersome so be careful where you place them. Avoid excessive contrast between the light intensity in the work zone and out of it for strong contrasts strain the eyes. The ideal solution is adjustable illumination, easy to move around and to lower or brighten. The specifications will have to be even more precise if several different people use the same work zone.

It is not enough just to get the individual parts right; the overall result must be conducive to work. Indeed work can become pleasant.

Tables and chairs

Practical and comfortable. Tables and chairs are two essential elements for all work areas. Getting the furniture right, both the look and the

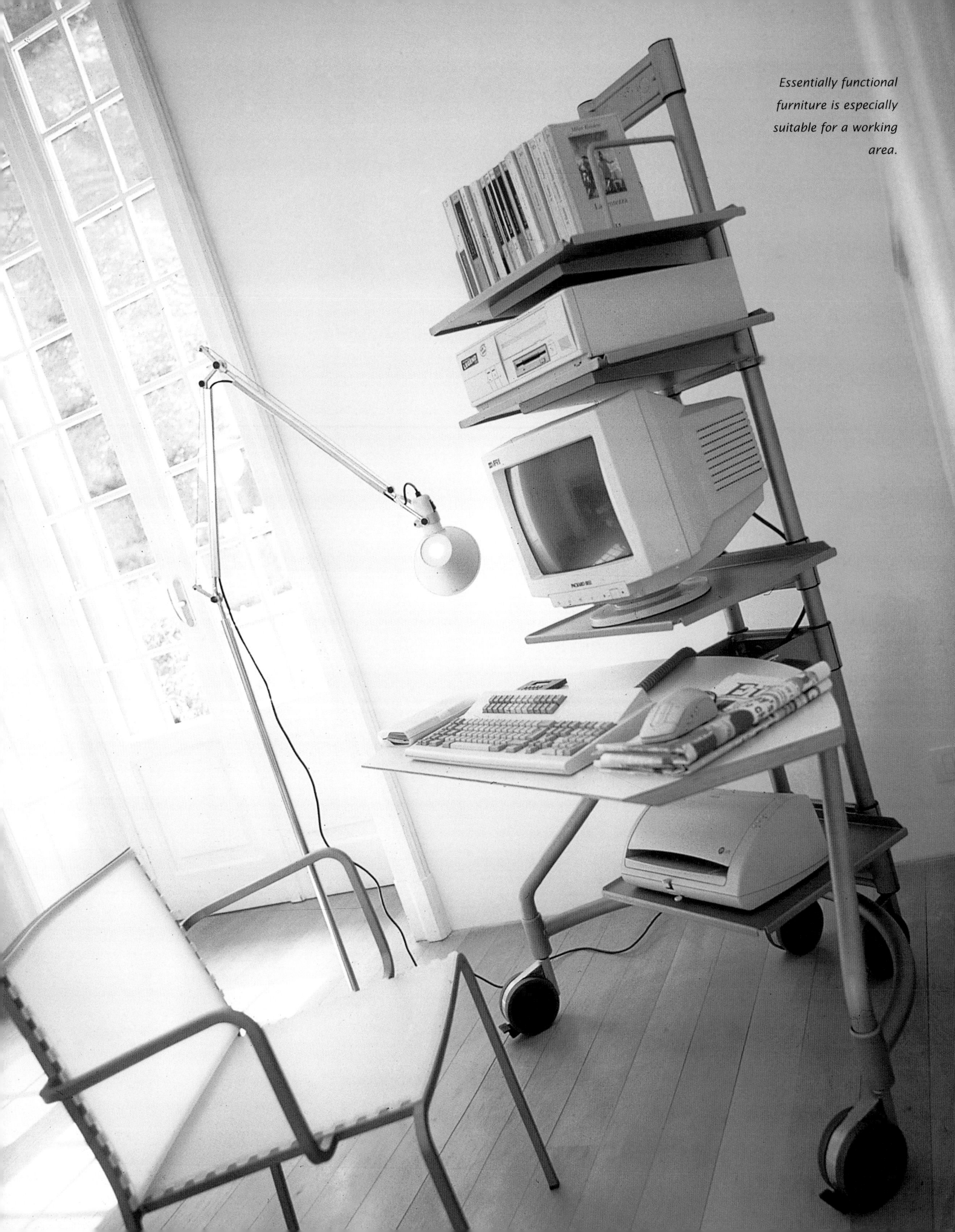

Essentially functional furniture is especially suitable for a working area.

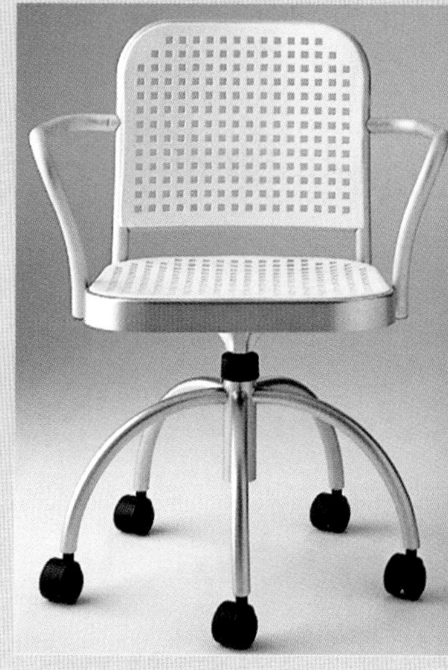

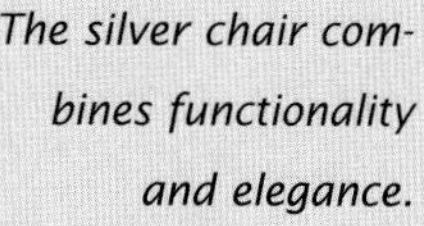

The silver chair combines functionality and elegance.

The ideal place for a study table is near to the window in the daylight.

Tables & chairs

practicality, is not an easy task.

The most important quality of a table is that it is big enough for us to work on and that it is the right height for us. Although it may appear that tables and chairs function independently, the choice of one heavily influences the other, unless we are thinking of using a height adjustable chair. Being comfortable when working greatly depends on the height of the chair and the table because we must be able to sit without stooping or straining our arms. Our mind will not be relaxed if our body is not. If the furniture is uncomfortable we will become tired and the work a grind. Ergonomic chairs specially designed for people who have to spend long hours sat at a desk are available in the market. In today's society, because of the benefits of e-commerce, some people now work out of their home and therefore comfort and tranquillity are even more primordial.

In loft residences and attics the office can be the most important part of the home. We can design a space as if it were a studio pushing the kitchen, the bathroom and the bedroom into the background. The office can double up as living room, and if the space is limited we can also eat there.

Making the space where we work feel open and bright is vital if we are to be at ease. Daylight, which tends to flood into these spaces, goes a long way in achieving this. Avoiding partitions is another aid. Even with an open plan style we can create different zones with distinct func-

Furniture with simple but elegant lines turns the study into a quiet and relaxed space.

The unusually shaped table provides welcome visual relief from our papers and files.

Books look scholarly and arouse interest. They can convert any corner into a study.

tions, while being aware of all that surrounds us. This will help us to feel comfortable.

Intelligently taking advantage of the furniture is crucial. Chairs, tables and book shelves will replace walls, dividing the space up into independent, interrelated zones.

Double height spaces, especially those that also have two floor levels, give good results with this type of project. Bookcases, photos and paintings can be hung on the high walls giving a clear style to all the room.

Special places

Delightful and unique. Some places have characteristics so unique that their charm soothes us so we decide to turn at least part of this space into a work area. Our professional responsibilities will become a pleasure.

Tidy and unobtrusive: limited space encourages improvisation in the corridor.

The characteristics or little twists of these places make them different. A wall with old, interesting or stimulating paintings or photographs, or neoclassic architectural features can serve as the starting point for a decoration program. As we are constructing, or decorating, starting from the charm of the special characteristics we must be careful not to spoil them in any way with what we do. The details must be perceived as before. Filling a room with antique furniture, paintings, prints, curtains or other decorative elements will only clutter it up and push

Restoring the nobleness of an old office area makes for uniquely alluring results.

Double height ceilings with a lot of light are ideal for studies.

its innate charm into the background. Choosing furniture with simple, modern lines will help us to differentiate the new elements from the old ones. Their simplicity will not get in the way of the general perception of the spaces and its details. Libraries and offices are personal spaces where we have to feel comfortable. However, they must have a striking look, with personality. Therefore these special places are ideal.

Special places

Isolation and concentration. When we decide on the space distribution of our home we can opt for placing the work area completely separated from zones for other activities. Should it have its own exclusive zone?

In small flats or houses finding a quiet study corner may be difficult for not all corners are valid. A work zone must be isolated so that we can concentrate, something not easy if people are constantly passing through. Maybe the bedroom is the best alternative because there is little transit. Setting up a desk, chairs and a lamp is no problem, but perhaps the storage space is harder to fit in. The corridor, a space without a clear function, can be turned into a practical, well decorated library.

Put color to work for nobody wants a sterile operating room look.

Organizing furniture

Ordered and balanced. A great volume of books and documents must be systematically stored or filed in offices, studios and libraries. Shelves, cup-

A space with neoclassic lines combined with modern furniture produces a moderately formal area.

Organizing furniture

boards and drawers are the means available to carry this out.

The choice of the most efficient storage system for our needs depends on what we have to store and the look we are seeking. If we like the image offered by libraries, books covering the walls forming a mosaic of colors and textures, we will employ a shelving system. If we want horizontal and vertical lines to stand out we can choose deep, wide shelves. Sleek metal or crystal shelves are more subtle and likely to go unnoticed. The books can be hidden and protected from dust at the same time behind little sliding doors. Glass doors remind us of old libraries or offices. However, we may choose sliding cabinet-like doors for a reason other than image: they are ideal for enabling us to place a book case in any part of the home.

Drawers are not practical for books but they are very useful for keeping documents, compacts and other small items which need to be protected from the dust. We do not have to be limited to the shelves sold in the shops. Using a little imagination we can come up with original storage systems made from unexpected materials. A long, narrow table backed up against a wall holds piles of books. A home-made shelving system is produced by placing wooden planks between old bricks. Any little ledge is a shelf to be taken advantage of, provided that the effect created is ordered.

Daylight and color enable us to have a neat and unified space.

Creating an ambience

Specific lighting

Like the other decoration ingredients, light enables us to modify the perception of the spaces and to create an attractive ambience. To complete a good decoration program it is essential to be aware of the possibilities.

Lighting

Working lamps

New design

Placing several lamps strategically is the key to good scenic lighting.

Creating an ambience

One atmosphere.

When creating a lighting program it is necessary to start at a general level before getting down to details. This will ensure that we achieve a unified and balanced ambience. Firstly weigh up the possibilities permitted by the electrical supply. If it does not have sufficient power for the lamps and spotlights we are planning to install it will have to be refitted.

Determining the quantity of light necessary for each area requires precise attention. Analyze the activities to be carried out in each space, calculating approximately how much light is necessary. Adjustable lighting which allows us to change the light source and the power of the bulbs, using free standing lamps and spotlights if needed, are extremely useful.

To light any space two concepts can be applied, either independently or working together. General lighting is more for aesthetics than for practicality. Its objective is to illuminate the space in such a way that it appears unified. In small spaces it gives good results because it makes them appear bigger. The general illumination need not be practical. Although it is useful for certain things we do, above all socializing, it is insufficient for reading, cooking, drawing, etc. The most imaginative and creative solutions are hit upon when we combine the general lighting with spotlights and lamps. This produces very adaptable ambiences.

Steen lamp

Alvar lamp

Dualada lamp

Tronkonil lamp

Short armed BC3 lamp

G5 tripod lamp

Weighted lamp

Fuchsia lamp

Decent lighting confers a special atmosphere and coherence on a space.

A simple lamp on a table creates an alluring corner.

Specific lighting

To the point and practical. Specific lighting must be both alluring and practical. Aesthetically it enables us to divide the space, making it seem smaller and, at the same time to create focus points. On the practical level it is this lighting which enables us to do specific things like studying and reading.

Scenic lighting, always highly decorative, has the capacity to focus attention on certain points or objects, bringing to the forefront what we want to stand out, like, for example, an antique piece of furniture, a sculpture or a painting. Theatrical, dramatic lighting is suitable for moving them center stage. The shadows cast and the attractive, suggestive tones and nuances created depend on the relative position of the light source and the object illuminated. Table lamps and free standing lamps are indispensable if we want flexible, effectual lighting. They are easily moved around and adapt to different situations. Another advantage is that they do not need to be pre-installed, just simply plugged in and placed in the right place to get the light needed. Their decorative contribution is twofold. Their very appearance can be stimulating, a sleek minimalist design for example, and secondly the light they produce can be evocative. Shades prevent the light from dazzling us and go down well anywhere. Lights should not be placed in transit zones or where children play for they could be knocked over accidentally.

Working lamps

Functional and attractive. In work areas like studies and libraries the aesthetic side of the lighting is somewhat displaced by practical considerations. This does not mean that we forego the decorative influence of the illumination, rather the functional aspect comes to the fore.

Ceiling lighting is not recommended for these rooms. It is acceptable for the general lighting but in specific areas can

A collection of lamps with shades and wooden bases

The Gira lamp

Bloc lamp

Cone lamp

Scenic lighting creates distinct focuses of attention without destroying the idea of unity.

Functionality and aesthetics come together in the new concepts of work lamps.

Working lamps

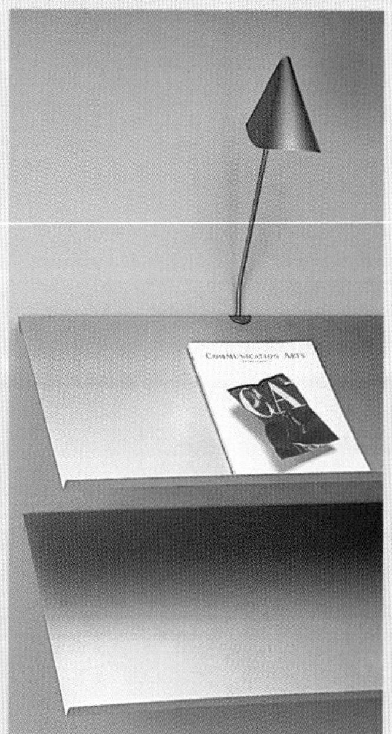

Lamps add style.

throw annoying shadows onto the work area. Among the benefits gained from table lamps and wall lights is that they can be placed near the work zone and, normally, their height can be adjusted. Flexibility is a big plus for all types of necessities.

The light sources must be precisely located to make working easier. Light should hit the pages of a book at 20º. If this angle is lower the skimming light produces bothersome shadows.

However, some activities are carried out more comfortably with shadows as they give contrast and aid vision. Some shades create a dividing line along the shadow's edge. It should be at eye level so that the bulb does not dazzle us.

The quantity of light required for a work zone oscillates between 150 and 300 lux, depending if it is going to be used for long periods or only occasionally. However, it is not merely necessary to get sufficient light for the study area: another consideration is for there not to be an excessive contrast with the surroundings to avoid eye strain. A rough guide is one third of the light intensity of the work zone.

Lux is a unit used to measure the illumination. The lamps and bulbs sold in the market should have this reference marked and thus help us in our calculations. Otherwise we will have to fall back on the watts stated.

Combining general lighting with spotlights gives the best results in large areas.

New designs

Curious and original. The world of design has seen that lamps and light sources in general offer potential for expression. Light's properties mean that it is a basic decoration tool and one of special interest. Controlling it and molding it has given the designers a lot of scope.

New technologies have made themselves felt in the illumination field. Fibre optic, neon tubes and low consumption bulbs have widened the horizons. The market offers solutions for each and every one of our practical necessities, while at the same time being compatible with strictly aesthetic considerations.

Lamps went from being mere providers of light to become engaging, seductive models only allowed into our homes if they passed the good taste filter. A design table lamp is comparable to a sculpture of light, an aesthetic object to please our senses. The new decoration trends are getting the most out of light to emphasize the creativity of other items forming part of the creative process. Light is necessary to perceive the space and, simultaneously, it is part of the decoration in its own right. Light attracts us irresistibly. Any lamp or light source inevitably becomes a focus of attention, and even more so if it is style conscious and innovative.

Design and technology work together to create new lamp concepts.

Materials and colors work together in the bedroom to create imaginative ambiences.

The lighting gives new forms of decorative expression.

Lighting dresses the architecture.

ngenious solutions

Accessories

The magic and the delight of water make the bathroom a special refuge. Mirrors, lights, tiles and chrome taps form a practical but enchanting space.

Bathrooms

Brightness and colo

New designs

Design has created novel and attractive solutions for the bathroom.

Ingenious solutions

ngenious solu

Precise and creative.
Bathrooms are spaces in which great care is dedicated to the small details because many functions are carried out in this limited area. The bathroom is a sanctuary where we get ready to face the world so practicality and comfort are at a premium.

Normally toilets and bathrooms are small spaces so we must take care with the decoration, maximizing the creativity and ingeniousness, to find practical and solutions which look good.

The principal function of a bathroom is to provide us with a place where we can look after our personal hygiene, from taking a bath through to washing and shaving. If we have enough space we can install a traditional bath, a hand basin, a toilet and a shower unit. This formula tends to opt for small-scale solutions which give the maximum independence to each of the zones. Plate-glass curtain walls divide up the space without making it smaller. If we want privacy, the solution is acid-etched glass which is translucent.

The traditional idea of a shower has been replaced by a new formula.

Pure contemporary bathroom formulas stop short of nothing. The most illustrative example is placing the hand basin outside of the bathroom, in a cupboard, behind some curtains or even out in the open. It has become another decorative element in the bathroom scheme. It is a great blessing to have natural light in the bathroom, even though it

Materials and colors work together in the bathroom to create imaginative ambiences.

Accessory furniture takes on pure, conceptual forms.

will not be sufficient for shaving. Light bulbs around the mirror, like in the dressing room of a theater, avoid shadows on the face. In the case that there is insufficient natural light we will have to ensure the general lighting is plentiful. Halogens bulbs produce cold, clean light, ideal for bathrooms. The shininess goes well with the mood.

Accessories

Practical and decorative. As we already said, the bathroom is essentially a practical space but it is important that attractiveness and style are not pushed aside. The complements will help us to this end.

Many different types of objects are stored in the bathroom: towels, soap holders, eau de toilette, shaving implements, etc. A practical, easy access storage space is called for. We do not have to rely on the classic formula of little wall cabinets above or below the sink. There are more ingenious solutions. We are spoilt for choice if we look for little cupboards on wheels and drawers. If we have limited space, cabinets on the wall leave other spaces free. Stackable furniture is another solution, as are metal shelves.

However, the list of accessories does not finish here: a series of complements are must haves in the bathroom. We cannot do much without looking in the mirror, and today even the mirrors can be admired on their own merit as they frame our reflection. Some of them have engravings. The market does not leave us stuck for choice.

Bathroom accessories include ring and bar towel holders, soap dishes, toilet paper holder, ledges and hangers, all of them aimed at making life in the bathroom more practical. These elements are necessary even inside the shower unit: hand rails and soap dishes are very useful.

Accessory furniture decorates the bathroom and gives us storage space.

Fun and imaginative chests of drawers convert the bathroom into a practical space.

Curtains, bath rugs, a stool and a little ledge are not vital but can add to our comfort. Their role is half way between being useful and adding attractiveness. Wall lights or lamps above the mirrors are also essential to get the illumination right.

Brightness and color

Color is especially meaningful in the bathroom.

Luminous and lively.
In the bathroom light is important if we need to shave or make up. Few people have the privilege of enjoying views from their bathroom window. However, if we are so lucky the window will become the leading player in the decoration program. If the window is only small, or simply there is not one, we must be careful that the lighting is decent so that the space is not cold and dark. Daylight makes the space more welcoming because of its invigorating powers. Color is the other key to making the bathroom as elegant as it is functional. Blue and green, fresh, relaxing colors, and white, clean and luminous, are heavily endorsed for bathrooms. Do not rule out yellow, a color that brings energy and life to the space. It combines particularly well with blue. Beige and cream natural tones are also suitable. They have white's luminosity and are summery and natural.

Natural light is a luxury which makes this space inviting.

Although halogens lighting fits well, other solutions are feasible. Neon tubes produce a cold, clean light, without shadows. However, they are relatively out of favor for homes becomes their image has been tarnished by heavy use in industry. Hidden in the ceiling cladding, however, they look good and give great practical results.

The electrical wiring must be safe in the bathroom for water can get everywhere. Before it would have been unthinkable to place lights above a bath tub but today there are halogens lamps specially designed for this end. Sockets and switches should follow the basic rule of being kept away from water.

Bathrooms are no longer places just to do the business. They must be elegantly proportioned, practical, comfortable and attractive.

New designs

Attractive and functional.
Investigation into bathrooms has hit upon a number of fetching solutions without forgetting that the bathroom is a place to relax and to cleanse oneself.

Stainless steel has caught on in modern bathrooms.

Wood and crystal can be boldly used in the bathroom.

New designs

The traditional bathroom has lost ground to the new designs.

Stainless steel pieces and chrome furnishings have come into their own in the new bathroom tendencies.

Glass hand basins have gained in popularity pushing ceramic ones out of the limelight. Design seeks to break away from tired ideas and traditions and to come up with new concepts and ways of understanding the bathroom in which aesthetics are as important as practicality.

Marble and tiles are also feeling the pressure of new designs, which in turn are harking back to nearly forgotten techniques like tempered stucco. Another curiosity is that wood, before considered unsuitable for the bathroom, is coming into fashion. These new materials and new uses mean that new solutions are necessary for toilets and bathrooms. Suspended toilets and bidés have gained ground on more traditional forms as the old image of bathrooms fades away into the past. The faucets are changing too. The models coming directly out of the wall have made a comeback and new applications appear on the market. The feeds which lead into basins and showers may be hidden. Shower cubicles are found less often. Today the shower is often conceived as a wider space closed off with plate-glass, sometimes etched, curtain walls. They are spaces designed for modern living.

New elements are also being introduced by the new tendencies within the rustic style. The bathroom is now a space suitable for holding items before only seen in other rooms of the residence, paintings, old furniture and little things like flowers and candles. As the bathroom is the place where the effects of the world are washed away, the decoration must be attractive as well as practical.

HOLA

Dressing rooms

Choosing a wardrobe

Original ideas

The necessity to store objects neatly has led to the creation of clever design furniture for a new type of space. Today the fashion of taking advantage of space to install a cupboard is in vogue.

Storage

Practical ideas

Dressing rooms

Separate and ordered.

Dressing rooms are designed exclusively for storing clothes, shoes bags and suitcases. Such a practical role could lead one to forget about aesthetical aspects, but this does not necessarily have to be so. Dressing rooms can make a great visual impact depending on how we arrange the objects therein.

The secret to obtaining an efficiently ordered dressing room is the planning. We have to analyze the objects that are going to be stored and how we can sort them. The less we use something, the higher up we could store it, even though a ladder may be necessary to get at it again. Boxes and paper wrapping will help to protect them from dust but will mean that what each packet contains will have to be written on the outside. This is probably the best place to store the out of season clothes. It could also be kept in the attic as we will not need it for several months. Garments and items we use once in a while can also be put on coat hangers. If we put them out of the way we will have more space for the objects used daily. Classifying the objects into different zones can be useful.

Be sure to have a separate zone for the bags and shoes because as they are made of leather their smell should not impregnate the clothes. Our clothes for every day must also be classified and a space designated for each type. Bear in mind that coats and dresses are longer than shirts or blouses, while other clothes are better off stored folded neatly and placed on shelves. Intimate clothes look good tucked away inside drawers, and maybe we need a zone for dirty clothes and what has to be ironed. Sorting by color or clothes type will certainly help us to find things in a hurry.
Order and classification are vital to make the dressing room a practical space.

Dressing rooms are practical areas. However, aesthetics must not be neglected and have to fit in with the rest of the home.

A fanlight converts this dressing room into a luminous, pure lined space.

The dressing room can be hidden behind sliding doors.

A cupboard covering an entire wall creates a neat effect.

Choosing a wardrobe

Choosing a wardrobe

Sliding doors are the perfect solution for getting the most out of the space.

Ordered space. It is not easy to choose the best system for storing our clothes. It is a decision taken very much in the light of how much space we dispose of and the way it is distributed.

Some large bedrooms offer us the possibility of creating a small dressing room which does not need doors because it is totally independent from the rest of the room. Less space available means that we will opt for cupboards, some of them maybe built in to the walls.

To avoid breaking the regularity of the space we will try to ensure that they cover entire walls. If there is the risk that the wardrobe makes the room look too small, acid-etched glass doors are a valuable resort. Sliding doors are the best solution for tiny rooms.

The dressing room does not have to be in the bedroom; it could be a transition space between the bedroom and the bathroom. A passage with a designated purpose.

Getting the lighting right in the dressing room is as important as in other parts of the home. Halogens lights produce an illumination quite similar to daylight. This would enable us to see the clothes' colors as if we were outside. The scenic lighting must be carefully placed because the shelving casts shadows on the clothes make it harder to distinguish their colors. Spotlights and wall lights are the best way round this problem.

The dressing room can be conceived as an independent space.

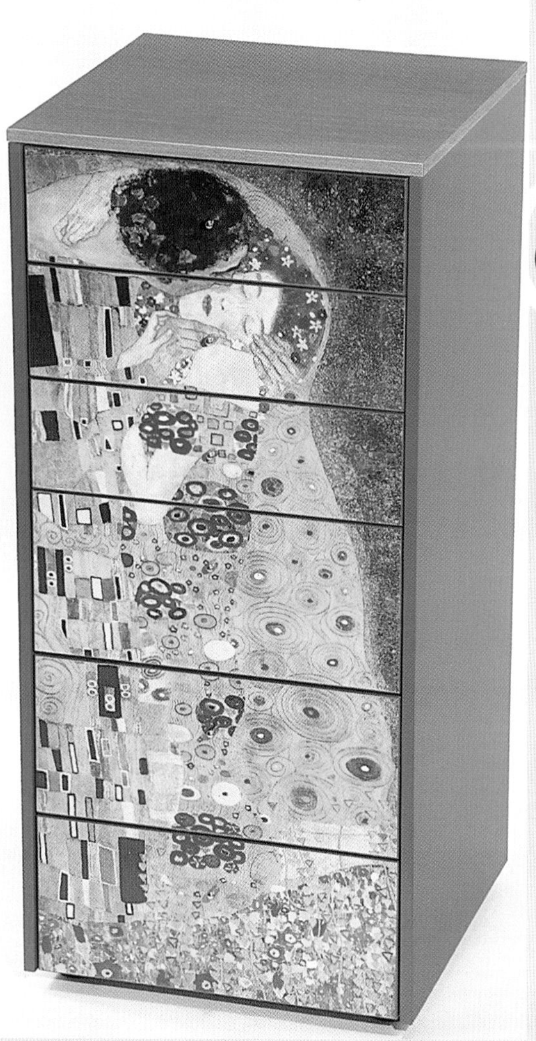

A chest of drawers is both a storage space and an element of decoration.

Original ideas

Original and practical.

Any corner of the home is fit for being converted into a storage area. Putting objects away does not have to be a boring chore or one which makes the section of the home in question ugly. The shops offer all sorts of furniture for storage. Trunks, chest of drawers, cupboards and sideboards serve for this purpose. It is quite common to place a chest or sideboard in the hall, on the landing or in the corridor and then to fill it with things which have to be stored.

Built in closets and attics enable us to make the most of the space. Often corridors and halls have unexploited corners where the space is wasted. Fitted furniture is a good way of putting this space to work. If there is a false ceiling, store away objects infrequently used in this space. Another original solution is to buy closets that act as partitions for when we want to separate two zones, either partially or totally. If the space is big enough a large cupboard can be placed in the middle. To conceal the fact that it is a cupboard, we can camouflage it with sliding doors and subtle handles so that it is difficult to realize that it is a cupboard and not a paneled wall. The approach will be completely different if we want to give the storage zone a particular look. Old furniture or some artifact that makes it special can serve as the focus point for the decoration. A sideboard or glass-door bookcase attracts a lot of attention not only for the furniture itself but also for what it contains.

Whatever option we choose, we must ensure that the storage system forms pa of the decoration.

Practical details

Stylish and practical.

The furniture allows us to combine thes two characteristics together.

Furniture designers have hit upon creative solutions for all necessities. If we are aiming at getting away from traditional formulas we are sure to find means of doing so. Bedrooms, dining rooms and living rooms all need a zone specifically for storage, or a piece of fur niture for this purpose. In the dining room a cupboard for the crockery, glass ware and tablecloths is useful because it means we do not rob space from the kitchen.

In the living room we should set aside a area to act as a library, in which to store

A piece of pure lined, imaginative furniture.

Cupboards can double as dividers. An idea especially suitable for minimalist styles.

Organize your domain: put the corners to work when space is scarce.

books, compacts and other objects. If necessary it can act as a storage overflow for the dining room. Any office or study the home may have will need some storage furniture, though its aspec can be informal, for documents and papers. A mini-chest of drawers on wheels or a filing cabinet that can be moved around or hidden under a table or in a corner are great ideas. In the bed rooms a whole range of objects have to be stored, from books through to clothes so the space has to be intelligently divid-ed up and organized. Bedroom furniture tends to be very practical, lots of drawers and shelves. However, if we have a traditional bed with bedside tables maybe we are going to need some accessory furniture, like cupboards. Beds with sliding drawers underneath come in handy if space is limited.

Practical details

Thinking of all the details will make our life more comfortable.

In small homes the corridors and halls can be used for storing items from differ-ent rooms. These spaces are easily accessed from all the home and normally they do not have a defined purpose. A bookcase in the corridor, built in closets in the hall or a sideboard in the corridor are all practical and elegant solutions.

Furniture is an important element of style, and the objects stored inside too.

An art gallery at hom

Other functions

These spaces are essentially transit zones between two rooms. Corridors and halls are ideal spaces to put into practice an independent decoration program.

Corridors

Light & colo

Welcome home

Decorative elements convert a dull corridor into an attractive space.

An art gallery at home

Elegant and interesting. Corridors are transition spaces without a clear function for no concrete activity is carried out in them. We move from one room to another. A decoration program that gives them character must be devised.

Art works, antique furniture and mementoes are ideal for this end. These objects have their own story and their own character and are therefore capable of bestowing interest on a zone. An attractive painting, maybe with bright colors, or a series of lithographs carefully laid out are a common resort. Sculptures, which have been discovered by less people, are especially attractive if adequately lit. Shadows can be thrown against the wall. Some antique furniture borders on being art work, or maybe it stands out for its singularity. However, furniture requires space so will not be suitable for every corridor.

The lighting of the corridor and the objects displayed require thought and study. Plentiful light is necessary because we move along the corridors and there must be no risk of tripping. Human eyes adapt slowly to contrast changes, so avoid irritating them. The light should not be markedly different from the rooms which lead into it. For example, if we use the corridor to go from a brightly lit dining room into a dark bathroom, the corridor will be a transition zone. Making a corridor interesting in its own right not only benefits the corridor but also the surrounding rooms. We should avoid allowing a dark, dull corridor be the com-

Some paintings make this hallway seem like a space with a clear role.

Original furniture is the center of attention and transforms a space.

If there is little space, a wide corridor leading to the dining room is an good place for a kitchen.

municating space in our home. Good decoration gets into all the corners of the house, spreading style and life uniformly. All the spaces in the home need to be coherently linked together, either directly or indirectly, and the corridor is one means of achieving this.

The hall and corridors of a residence present us with the challenge of creating a space that is compatible with all the rooms around it, thus unifying the decoration project in all the home.

Other functions

Funny and practical.

When we dispose of little space, the corridor can become vital. Maybe knocking down a wall means we have a bigger room and avoid a long, dark corridor, but this is not always possible. If we rule this option out we should consider giving the corridor its own function apart from merely being a zone we pass through. Perhaps the corridor can have a zone we have not been able to place in any other area of the home. A library is the most common use because it does not require a great deal of space. Shelves loaded with books breathe life into a staid corridor. Moreover, occasionally using this space as a library does not require a lot of daylight or room. If the corridor or hall is wide enough we could set up a little study or office area. In this case we would have to avoid that the people passing down the corridor put off the person working. Also adequate lighting would be necessary. This is not always easy so only try this suggestion out when the use would be occasional and not too many people live in the home. A corridor near a dining room is a good place to put a kitchen, which would require some basic illumination and ventilation conditions. Kitchens must always be practical and safe.

The spaces in our homes can be as adaptable as our imagination. The limits are imposed by creativity and the need to be practical.

An apparently useless corridor can be converted into an office or study.

Light and color

Bright and welcoming.

Corridors do not normally receive daylight directly meaning they could be gloomy if we did not install decent lighting. Often the illumination of corridor is overlooked. Both the colors of the walls as well as the lighting are essential to get a pleasing ambience. A visitor should feel

A library or bookcases in a corridor make it more interesting and give it personality.

comfortable in the corridor, and providing they are not being nosey, should want to carry on exploring the home. As we have already stated, dark, dull, boring corridors must be avoided and it is the decoration program which has the key role. Glowing colors are especially suitable for these spaces because artificial lighting intensifies the coldness of certain colors. Oranges and yellows will made a decently lit corridor a lively, animated space. We could even go as far as introducing red, there is no more vigorous color, onto the scene to give character.

Light & color

Light and color combine to make this corridor more interesting and stylish.

A curtain is one solution to separate the social area from the bedrooms.

If the corridor being decorated is too long or narrow, there are certain tricks to avoid this sensation. Color is one of them. Blue tones give a feeling of width. Breaking the corridor up into stretches, each one with different color will make it feel shorter. Or a curtain at the half way stage achieves the same effect. Lighting resorts can be added on top of color effects. Spotlights can be laid into the ceiling with switches at different points along the corridor. Then we can turn on or off the lights as we go along the corridor. The dark part of the passage will make the illuminated part seem shorter. Shadows and clarity can be played off against each other, emphasizing some parts of the corridor in comparison with others.

Ingeniously combining lighting and color effects will modify our sensation of space giving any corridor elements of interest in its own right for it, too, can be part of the decoration program.

This corridor has made the most of the space. It is a library and further on a kitchen counter or worktop has been installed.

Making the hall dramatic is permitted but it must be compatible with the rest of the living space.

If there is little space in the hall, the furniture will be removed and we will rely uniquely on the illumination and materials.

Welcome home

Welcoming and impacting. The hall is the first part of the home the visitor sees so it is eminently important what it tells the world about us and about our home.

If we view the hall as an essentially functional space, devoid of imaginative decoration, it will turn out a cold, uninviting space. One thing we must not do is clutter the hall up with too many objects because this could give an untidy sensation. A cupboard should be used for storing away coats, bags and umbrellas.

Old houses tend to have grand halls which can be too bleak. Some furniture and other details can overcome this sensation. The entrance is like the shop window of our home so we must make a few concessions if it is to be dramatic. Bright, glowing colors, lights contrasted with shadows and some flowers or artifacts will give more of a spring, rejuvenated feeling. In modern homes the halls tend to be smaller with a great multitude of doors leading off of them. In this case we will have to forego a lot of furniture, but we will be able to include a few twists like a hat stand or a coat hanger. Color and the lighting come to the front in this part of the house. The doors can be painted in engaging colors or intriguing free standing lamps, or ceiling lights, can be installed.

Country houses, or any home which has a hall that opens directly onto the outside, need to have a tough floor to stand up to the constant coming and going. If the flooring did not match the rest of the home, we could use a rug or a door mat. Not only are they useful for protecting the floor, avoiding dirt being brought in, but also they warm the space up, add style through their textures and decoration patterns. Entrances offer a sample of the style of the rest of the house, what lies beyond the threshold, so the ambience must be in accordance.

Cupboards are extremely useful for keeping the hall neat and tidy.

"Less is more"

Color and forr

Architecture and decoration combine to create ambiences in which the elements are reduced to the minimum seeking pure expression. The decoration gives a radical twist to the concept of these spaces.

Minimalism

apanese influences

Furniture elegance

"Less is more"

Pure and essential. A new way of conceiving spaces has started to influence decoration; a new dimension has been added. Addition has been pushed aside by subtraction: the objective is to reduce as much as possible. Knowing what are the minimum elements necessary to create a functional and practical ambience is the key to the minimalist tendency.

The tendency in decoration was imported from art. However, in the latter the results were even more conceptual because art does not have the practical restraints imposed on interior design.

Creating a comfortable and functional space reducing the elements to the essential minimum expression is more than jus a question of austerity. A detailed and exhaustive analysis of the necessities, materials and aesthetic possibilities is an essential step, but not the only one. Minimalism is strongly conditioned by the surroundings and seeks to use them to bring out the best of the residence. As minimalism takes so many things away, the daylight takes on a greater role modeling the space and creating ambiences. New technologies and materials also come into play to obtain the maximum expression with the minimum gesture and elements.

Understanding the space is a fundamental step when developing a design process. The forms are rigorously defined and pure, the surfaces smooth. In these ambiences the furniture is at its most expressive, in some cases turning almost architectural.

The decoration details are also reduced to the minimum giving them a new expression. Knowing at which point the minimum is sufficient is the key to this new decoration concept.

Some images could make us uncertain as to whether these spaces are comfortable and functional. With their hand lines these spaces seem conceived only for their aesthetic virtues. However, although it is difficult to get an equilibrium between aesthetics and functionality it is possible.

When the decorative elements are minimum, natural light is even more potent.

Sense of style: materials and forms, too, are decoration.

The forms are essential to define the space.

What has to be avoided is that the look steam rolls over the practicality and spaces to be admired are created instead of spaces to be lived in.

Color and form

Formal and welcoming. Minimalist ambiences do not forget about the principals and resorts of traditional decoration, though it does apply them subject to a new aesthetic and formal concept. Color becomes highly important when the elements are reduced to the minimum and its qualities of expression take on a new dimension. Painting walls and ceilings modifies the perception of the spaces as they develop their own character. Glowing yellow and red tones warm up spaces that may be cold because of the basicness of the elements. Greens and blues create relaxing, harmonious ambiences which soften hard lines and geometric forms. White and neutral tones emphasize the forms and intensify the purity of the daylight. As the decorative elements are minimized the forms become the protagonists. Geometry comes into play as it relates the objects in the space, converting walls and openings into almost structural features. The shadows and lights are another part of the decoration in which the designer must find a balance between the minimalist concept, the rationality of the space, functionality and comfort. Forms and colors are essential tools for getting the right aesthetic and poetic balance. The psychological effects of colors are an important ally for making sparse interiors more joyful and light hearted. The forms model the spaces, adapt them to our necessities and seek beauty and style, so elusive and desirable.

Colors make the space more comfortable and welcoming.

Controlling the decorative recourses and applying them to the minimalist concept will create a stylish pure lined ambience, yet cozy and functional.

Japanese influences

Natural and comfortable. East meets West. Oriental influences have reached our culture and made themselves felt in our homes, increasing the expression and lightening the look with their pure forms and materials. During centuries far off countries like Japan and China impacted on the world of art and culture, and now on decoration. Empha-

This space gets its energy from the warmth of the color yelow.

Japanese influences

sizing the purity of the spaces and forms fits well with the minimalist principles, although in the oriental culture it is more natural and poetic. Oriental aestheics seek to evoke expressive images compatible with functionality.

It is typical for these spaces to be in contact with outdoors, maximizing the contact with nature and using warm materials. Elements very characteristic of the oriental culture like futons and sliding wood and paper doors are powerful decorative recourses for creating ambiences. Neutral, natural tones are preferred for these calm, quiet spaces. Another constant factor is the quest for equilibrium: dividing up the space and the elements is essential if the area is to be relaxing. Meditating about what is important in life is a basic part of the Japanese culture, reflected in the purity of the compositional lines. Finding the meeting point of aesthetics, functionality and mystery is basic step for creating harmonious and balanced spaces. Gardens are the maximum expression o the oriental influence on the exteriors. Pure and essential lines let nature do th rest. Although the forms come across, the contents are lost. In a Japanese garden every element has its meaning, converting the area into the ideal place for meditation. Importing these models into our culture implies that something of their values, the origin of such pure and seductive forms, comes with them. Taking advantage of forms and recourse from other cultures is enriching and can be the pretext for the creation of singular and imaginative ambiences.

Pure lines and simple details reveal the Japanese influence.

Furniture elegance

Imposing and fundamenta

Purity and specification exist not only in the spaces but also in the elements. Furn ture becomes supremely important in the decoration when there is little that takes the attention away from it. One of the basic principles of minimalism is to reduce the number of elements until only the essential remains. This affects the furniture, too. Not only is the number of objects reduced, but also they are reduced to their minimum expression. The fur niture is straight lined and geometric, almost structural. Its value is not only functional but also aesthetical. The furnishings are configurative. When the architectural elements are minimized the use of support elements becomes necessary to divide the space into zones. Furniture is specially suitable for this function.

The furniture moves to center stage, almost like sculptural elements.

Furniture elega

Minimalist furniture is imposing and elegant with pure lines and rigorously defined shapes. It is another component of the space. The objective of the design is to get the austere furniture to be cozy simultaneously. Minimalist aesthetics do not mean that it must be forgotten that creating inviting spaces where living is a pleasure is the main aim of design and decoration.

Moderation and elegance come from the materials. Using natural materials ensures the quality of the furniture and bestows the integrity of nature on the warm ambience. However, new materials have also come into fashion. Steel, aluminum and even plastic are ideal materials for creating pure and geometric forms so, logically, they are in vogue.

Classic and modern styles are blended together under the sway of minimalism to produce extraordinarily elegant furniture which gives flavor to the ambience. Minimalist sofas, beds, chairs and armchairs are halfway between furniture and sculptures, contributing at the same time to aesthetics and functionality. Only carefully thought out and designed pieces can meet the target.

Elegant furniture and the accessories give warmth to minimalist ambiences.

Simple lined furniture matches the simplicity of the minimalist spaces.

Recycling industrial

ncepts, the stair cas

Restoring old warehouses and factories and converting them into homes has given rise to a new formula: the loft. They are spaces that are beyond the traditional idea of homes and have allowed new concepts to be introduced into the living space.

Lofts

Light rules

Height put to good

High ceilings are a typical feature of these buildings.

Recycling industrial spaces

Attractive and imaginative. So many old industrial warehouses and factories in the cities and the desire to restore them have led to the birth of this new type of residence. These buildings have a singular and characteristic architecture which has caught the eye of decorators and interior designers keen to try out new decoration programs while respecting the pre-existing architecture. Designers are always on the look out for new opportunities and formulas, and thus this new type of dwelling came into being breaking with tradition and preconceived concepts about building use. Partitions and walls came down and open plan spaces moved in. Sometimes only the bathroom and kitchen are closed off spaces. The rest of the home is one unit with the emphasis on functionality.

Another plus for the designer who wants to create something special is that these buildings have superb roofs. Industrial architecture is renowned for roof structures with visionary vaults and beams. Nobody wanted to simply tear these valuable constructions done: what was necessary was a facelift, conserving the original beauty. Some roofs have become the protagonists, standing out against the simplicity of the rest of the space. Other roofs are integrated into the overall effect.

Skylights and fanlights are other common elements which enrich the design potential of these edifices. They have been painstakingly recovered and restored to form an integral part of the new dwelling. Light is attractive and when it flows in from overhead it creates a joyful, singularly charming ambience.

Industrial buildings often have high ceilings. The transformation into a comfortable living space has given the opportunity to create a new level, but always avoiding a radical destruction of the space's unity.

Usually the double height ceiling was left intact permitting communication between the two levels and giving freedom to the natural light which floods all the home. Architecture, decoration and the concept of space must complement each other and allow the merits of the original construction to remain. It is a question of enhancing and reconverting what was already there.

Skylights give us an ambience flooded with natural light.

Preserving the original features of the industrial architecture is representative of these spaces.

New concepts, the stair case

A metal stair case becomes an almost sculptural element.

Conceptual and innovative. Stair cases have a new significance in lofts. Old style stair cases would not fit into the singular architecture of these spaces with their high ceilings.

Stair cases are almost like sculptures due to the lack of walls. They become organizers of the space as they divide it up. If we are going to do away with the normal dividers, walls etc, we have to replace what we have subtracted. Stair cases make a great contribution.

Preconceived ideas about stair cases are gutted out. Stair cases in lofts are open and communicative structures that blend in without blocking the vision across the space. The materials, most frequently wood or metal but glass is coming onto the scene too, have to be carefully chosen to achieve this aim: pure structuralism. Bold ideas, exploiting form and rich daring color, can be put into practice with these new stair cases so that they are worthy of being the center of attention. A solid structure, daring colored steps or an unusual shape are some of the recourses.

However, maybe our intention is the opposite. We want the stair case to go unnoticed, integrating it in with the whole project. A metal structure reduces the elements to the minimum and glass steps will be transparently sophisticated.

The materials can integrate the stair case into the space we desire. If the two levels have different floorings, the stair case can use either one of them depending on where we want to integrate it. Inevitably the stair case creates a link, not just physically.

Traditional stair cases have no place besides the new, radical concept of the loft residences. The overriding principle is that the stair case is compatible with the global design and does not get in the way of the communication or the decorative expression.

This stair case is transparent but the reflected colors makes it stand out.

Light rules

Summery and inviting. Natural light streaming through the windows and skylights generously fills the space with glowing radiance.

Factories and warehouses normally have large windows in the walls and in the roof, offering a lot of scope for

The material permits us to establish a connection between the stair case and the upper level.

Light rules

Large windows allow in abundant light.

Natural light has the power to unify the spaces.

imaginative decoration. Fortunately, there is no alternative but to let light rule over the space with its tendency to unify and modify the perception. A property we must get the most out of. Another of its qualities is its feel-good factor. High ceilings and an industrial past could mislead us into shunning these type of edifices for their supposed coldness but if we regulate the natural light, filtering and screening a little, the sensation and perceptions can be entirely soothing. This quality is enhanced due to the absence of walls and partitions: light reaches every corner. When there are two floors the double ceiling space should be preserved so that no light is lost. Skylights, fanlights and ceiling windows open up a whole range of decoration possibilities and the spaces lit can be used for all types of activities, especially for a home office with the maximum specifications. Light makes the space seem bigger and more inviting. We will feel comfortable in it. It is also a great place for a large, open kitchen and could even share the space with the dining room, or an informal but practical living room.

Open spaces with generous lighting were sure to make a success of the loft concept.

Height put to good use

Spacious and bright. The loft concept of space is ideal for young people and for not-too-large residences. Knocking down the walls produces a sensation of continuity and openness, the spaces seem bigger.

These projects require even more careful planning than traditional homes because the techniques which permit the maximum expression in decoration are put into practice as we do away with the dividers. As we already mentioned, the high ceiling allows us to create a second level, very suitable for the bedroom. It will be intimate but not separated from the rest of the residence. Below it the two rooms of the home that need a certain amount of individuality are placed: the kitchen and the bathroom. A low ceiling enables us to close them off but without sacrificing the unity of all the space. The stair case joining the two spaces must

Such plentiful natural light brings outside indoors.

High ceilings mean that the natural light can be taken advantage of.

leight put to good use

Open plan floors that communicate visually are especially characteristic of lofts.

have its own character, somewhat differentiated from the previous structure. The recourses used in a space that does not permit the creation of a second level are distinct. In this case the furniture is our most powerful tool for zoning the space without destroying its unity. Grand cupboards which do not reach the ceiling will give independence to the bedroom, although they will not be necessary if we have planned a totally open space. Only the bathroom has to be separate but if there is plentiful natural light and we want this to reach into the bathroom we can use glass bricks, or acid-etched curtain walls and tall windows. If we are after a more daring look we can leave some part of the bathroom, like the basin or bath tub, in the living space. It will take on an aesthetic and decorative function as it integrates into a project thrown together in a seemingly effortless way. Lofts are normally accommodation for one or two people so the need for intimacy is relative.

The kitchen can be totally open to the rest of the home. We will lay aside traditionalism and conceive a kitchen capable of being integrated into the rest of the living space. Constructing a kitchen that beguiles us will mean that it is easy to integrate into the space, be it with the dining area, the living zone, or even the office. Simple line furniture and reducing the elements to the minimum, but not forgetting functionality, will aid us. The eating area can be independent or integrated into the kitchen. A shortage of space would push us into using the dining table as a work area, or we can eat in the kitchen.

Chimneys play an important role in lofts because of their capacity to organize spaces and mark imaginary lines which distribute the elements. The living space must be functional, flexible and open, with the furniture marking off the zones according to functions.

Colors and materials can also be highly useful for zoning the space. A color throw or a change of material can indicate the edge of one space without the need for formal partitions.

The concepts and style applied to lofts is also worth employing on other types of spaces which need not be warehouses or grand, luminous buildings. The essence of these projects is to distribute the space relegating the old concepts into the back-

Here the old ceiling beams have been maintained emphasizing the space and luminosity.

Height put to good use

The space has been organized into different visually communicated levels.

ground. It is a formula valid for small offices and studies. Space shortage means that flexible multi-functional rooms have to be created. Knocking down walls frees up space which does not have to be used for corridors or hallways giving a more open plan and a sensation of more liberty.

Height opens up the door to new spaces.

This philosophy can also be applied to rooms used for different functions.

Using the furniture, the colors and the materials to mark off different zones will give clarity to the space. We must try to limit ourselves to what is necessary because it would be easy to fall into the trap of cluttering up precious space and forgetting our original intention.

The height of the ceiling has permitted an attic to be installed.

ding with natural lig

Stairways to the sky

Unique architectu

Close to the sky and full of radiant light, attics and lofts are unique spaces in which the decoration has total freedom to create comfortable dwelling places for life today.

Penthouses

Glass walls

A bird's eye view

Stone and wood,
natural materials,
warm up the space.

Leading with natural light

Full of radiant light, spacious and relaxing, attics, lofts and garrets are the spaces where the decorator and the dweller come closest to the sky. They are normally interrelated with the surroundings and are favored with magnificent views. In most cases the ceiling of the attics and lofts are sloped and the spaces are open plan, making them especially suitable for bold and innovative decoration projects. They are the ideal place in which to design a unique residence where daylight, flowing in through the roof windows, is inevitably a key protagonist. Other factors, like the architecture of the building, can also play a role in the decoration project. Wooden beams or bare walls can be the focus points that help to create a coherent and ordered decoration scheme.

Attics and lofts are full of openings, both in the walls and in the ceilings. Some are partly in the open air, if they have terraces or balconies. In fact, these elements must be the principal guides to the decoration program. As natural light floods into all the spaces, bringing them to life in a way impossible for artificial light, it has to be taken advantage of. If the living space has hardly any partitions, this radiance will reach into every corner providing a relaxing and cozy ambiance as bright as outside.

Windows open to the
sky allow in plentiful
sunlight.

ght

The wooden beams have become a decorative element.

The views through the windows are another protagonist: The blue of the sky is reflected in the colors. The spaces basked in this light seem fresh and tranquil.

Stairways to the sky

Stairways to the sky

Practical and decorative. In architecture staircases have a double role: they must be functional and yet at the same time be decorative. On many occasions they are the center of attention of a space, giving it structure and ordering it. Wood, glass, metal, steel, stone and marble are just some of the materials used to design staircases. They are key protagonists, vital to give character to the space and make our personal touch felt.

Light, sturdy, minimalist, a staircase can have distinct styles and forms. This will allow us to create a unique structure that tones in with the surrounding space and the tastes of the people who will ascend and descend. An alternative is to give the staircase a low profile. It can have fine lines or be almost transparent. This will increase the openness of the space.

The stair case fulfills its function and also decorates the home.

Apartments high up with two floors open up a whole world of architectural possibilities. One advantage is the communication between the two levels, related and independent simultaneously. The second consideration is that we need two floors if we are going to have a staircase.
The steps, the banister, and the handrail give us new decorative elements on which to work.

The oval shaped dining room is reached by a stair case which imitates its form.

The wooden structure casts interesting shadows onto the ceiling.

Daylight, or when it is lacking artificial light, is a key factor on the staircase. Good lighting will permit us to emphasize how much a well designed staircase can improve the decoration. The shadow of the steps can be cast on to the floor and the wall if the staircase is open. If it is closed, the light can illuminate the different planes. Light does not only play a role in making the space beautiful: it is also necessary to make it practical and comfortable. We must be able to see the steps. A dimly lit staircase can be dangerous for the users, as well as unattractive aesthetically.

Unique architecture

Attractive and warm. Attics and lofts are just below the roof so often the structure is uncovered, revealing curious architectural features. On modern buildings they may be rather dull, but on old constructions they have the attraction that only time gone-by can bestow. Intricate wooden beam, vaults, and arches are some of the architectural features that will play a part in the decoration, enriching the spaces and making them warmer and more welcoming.

Good quality materials become more alluring as they age. This is the patina of time on woodwork. The case of architecture is the same. Noble materials like marble, stone or iron, properly conserved are embellished over time. The doing up old buildings must always respect prominent, distinguished features of the old architecture. It is easy to turn them into decorative attributes.

Matching the ceiling off against the floor gives rhythm to the composition.

Where there is intense light , there are great views. Where else would you want to spend the afternoon reading.

The architectural and structural elements are other factors that add to the decoration. They give texture to the space. Just think about the shadows cast by wooden ceiling beams, or the uneven light projected onto a stone wall, with all its crevices. It will be difficult to find new architectural elements that enhance the space as much as these do.

Glass walls

Bright and communicative.

Attics and lofts enable us to create a feeling of openness using glass walls and large windows. The spacious terraces which these rooms can open out on to form part of the living space. The dimensions are increased. The close and ever present relationship with outdoors makes the spaces more relaxed, luminous and airy. We can sit down enjoying all the comforts of being simultaneously indoors and outdoors. The large windows allow us to gaze over the stunning views from our high vantage point. Although a room with floor to ceiling windows or glass walls may not seem very cozy due to the lack of textures or decorative features, spending some time there will soon make us realize that the surrounding landscape itself provides the decoration as it impacts on the mood. The views retain the sense of liberty from the contact with outside. They are the best picture that can be hung on the wall.

Glass walls establish close contact between inside and outside.

Spaces which open out on to terraces are specially suitable for doing activities like reading. Therefore, they are ideal to be used as studies, offices and libraries. The abundance of light that reaches into every corner will prevent us from straining our eyes.

However, not only aesthetics are important. These spaces have to be

comfortably insulated thermally and acoustically so it is important to carefully chose the structures that hold the glass in place. Traditional woodwork gives a warm feeling but it is a poor insulator. Iron window frames have the advantage of being thin, but they are somewhat heavy. In contrast, aluminum window frames are light but thicker. Our choice will depend on our necessities and the aesthetic effect we are seeking.

A bird's eye vie

A bird's eye view

Splendid views. Attics and lofts are on the upper floors of the buildings and therefore enjoy privileged views over the panorama. However, more important than the surrounding scenery in an attic is the sky, with its blue tones in spring, white and overcast on cloudy days, orangy in the Fall and gray on stormy days. The firmament projects its restlessly twinkling starry reflections on to the wall at night. During the day, too, the natural illumination changes as it warms up the ambiance.

These spaces must only have essential furnishings so that the views and the light are maximized. The furniture, too, must be as light and as unobtrusive as possible. Grand bookshelves or other bulky furniture are not recommended, unless there is a blind wall against which to place them. Do the layout always bearing in mind where we are going to be seated so that nothing gets in our line of vision.

Except in the bedrooms, where they are necessary for privacy, curtains are not normally used in this type of space. However, if you do decide to hang them, make sure that they do not get in the way of the windows when they are drawn back.

Another way of enriching the apartment is by placing plants and furniture on the terrace or balcony. Also visible from inside, they will add a touch of color. Avoid tall or thick plants so that there is no cluttering. The furniture, as is the case inside, must be minimum and as light as possible.
In spaces which draw on the landscape for their ambiance, the decoration can slip out of the limelight, but this does not mean that it should be neglected.

The city is laid out at your feet looking out from an attic.

The views in this attic are the decoration.

pace & harmony

Space and harmony

Equilibrium and unity. Decoration is much more than just distributing the furniture and objects in a space. The character of a space depends on its form, size and the light, three ingredients which come into play when deciding on the decoration. And, of course, we must take into consideration our tastes and necessities.

Some of the features of the space itself can help us. For example, a chimney would undoubtedly become the center of attention for organizing the room. This means that other parts of the space are pushed into the background. However, it is up to us what must stand out and what must be low-key. The decoration is our means to ensure that the result is pleasing. The illumination, the colors, the materials and the styles can all be worked on to give a harmonious and balanced space.

A chimney and a sofa are enough to create a cozy corner in which to relax.

The togetherness of the project must come before individual elements. A piece of furniture in one style may be out of tune with the other pieces around it. When choosing any fitting we have to be aware of how it is going to blend in with the ambiance and the style of the space.

Balancing openness and occupied space is equally important. The elements must be distributed around the space so that they do not invade or bunch each other. The activities of the room should be unhindered for functionality and comfort are as imperative as the aesthetics.

The ideal solution is a space in which we feel comfortable and can move around without tripping. It is a mistake to try and copy styles and ambiences. Everybody has their own style, identity, and tastes, all of which are going to be reflected in the space. For the visitor the appearance of our flat speaks volumes about what we are like. Therefore it must be expressive and communicative, qualities bestowing warmth, harmony and order.

The vaulted ceiling gives this room a special feel.

Objects & little details

Objects and little details

Ingenious and decorative. Decoration means a lot more than making an impact with the general concept. It is just as important to find the exact space for every object if we are to get a harmonious, coherent global feel. Neatness and order transmit equilibrium and harmony.

Over our lives we accumulate many things that we have to store in our homes so storage cupboards, whether hidden away or visible, are essential.

The kitchen par excellence is a room where all sorts of objects end up being stored. Some of them could never be described as beautiful so it is better to put them out of sight. However, other articles can be displayed as if they were decorative objects. A collection of jars or pots can liven up a kitchen or dining room.

Another touch of color or originality can be provided by flowers or fruit with their bright colors radiating energy, recalling nature and softly filling the air with their fragrance.

Books are another way of adding a personal feeling to the space. A mosaic of carefully arranged books, varying in size, color and texture, makes a strong impact on the surrounding space.

Although we may be aiming at a pure aesthetics or minimalist ambiance, we must remember that small details are essential

Color introduces something that breaks the monotony of the composition.

Works of art give character to a place.

to give a space personality. The way we spread some cushions or a blanket over a sofa, or the form used to tuck a curtain away, all of these are little details that add up to give the final result. Lit candles, a bunch of freshly picked flowers, and a burning fire are little give-away signs that tell the visitor we care about our home and are prepared to dedicate time to it.

Bookcases organize and separate the space.

Dashes of color

Suggestive and daring. A musical composition can have a discordant note and, in the same way, color allows us to introduce elements that clash with the overall harmony. When we try to make a space coherent or to unify the style, it is easy to fall into the trap of making it boring or monochromatic. Alternatively, as time passes, what before seemed sufficiently interesting to be the center of attention may now seem dull, stimulating us into introducing a new element. Sometimes the process goes in the opposite direction when we discover in a market an object sufficiently interesting to break the monotony of a tired or insipid room.

People evolve and their homes evolve with them. When planning a decorative program, you must always leave it open to changes. Moving furniture around or introducing something new can break the monotony.

There is no doubt that color is the most powerful means for introducing small changes. A colored piece of furniture can easily become the center of attention, breaking with the surrounding tones. Just like antic furniture, these colored pieces need to be selected with care and good taste. They must be placed in the right place. Sometimes a chair or an armchair may be badly placed but the mistake is covered up by the overall arrangement. However, if the furniture is a vivid color the problem is magnified and could spoil the whole effect.

Furniture on wheels makes the kitchen more versatile.

A collection of art works is the center of attention.

Works of art are most suitable for introducing a striking element into the scheme. The colors and forms are inevitably attractive to our eyes. We can gaze at them, trying to understand the details. Photographs and reproductions work in a similar way and they are more accessible price-wise, although they contribute less aesthetically to the space.

Taking over the space

Taking over the space

Personal and original.

Our personality is reflected in the way we dress and in the way we decorate our home. The work of an interior designer or decorator is not based on choosing objects to adorn somebody else's home. This is a widespread mistake. The interior designer must advise and help, always avoiding imposing their tastes. Their role is both to help with practical aspects and with aesthetics, being the ideal people to inform us about the possibilities available and how they adapt to our necessities. They can help us to solve technical problems and, if necessary, help us to choose particular items. Just as we would not feel comfortable wearing clothes chosen by someone else, in the same way we would not feel comfortable living in a space decorated according to another persons taste.We must leave our mark on the space, make it our own and reflect the way we are. Only then will it be more pleasant, cozy and functional for our needs. When we enter a well decorated home, straightway we realize that it tells us many things about the people who live there. A house full of pictures or sculptures will immediately make us think that the owner is a lover of art. Straight lines and geometric shapes will reveal their taste for rationalism. Small details are equally important in giving an image to the visitor. A cushion or bunch of flowers imaginatively placed will confirm to the visitor that we take an interest in decoration and care how our home looks. Decoration is, like all art forms, a medium of expression and communication. If we know how to wisely use the tools it offers us, we will be able to achieve pleasing results and get more out of our home.

The decoration reveals the tastes of the people who live there.

Old furniture

Restoring walls & ceilings

Natural, warm and sophisticated. Country styles take the best of the old traditions and modernize them to give cozy spaces, the attractiveness of which does not fade with time.

Country style

Colors & textures

Old furniture

Style and ambiance. Old furniture, whatever its style, has a marked character. This means it is ideal for giving personality to the space decorated, especially when you want to recreate an epoch. It takes us back in time evoking images and customs from the past.

To correctly choose a piece of antique furniture you must bear in mind the ambiance and the other furniture in the space. As they are markedly characteristic they are difficult to combine together, above all if they are of different styles. However, there are people who have a special sensibility for combining them and get stunning results. For those of us who do not set the standard so high, the best idea is to let the old furniture be the protagonist and to organize the other pieces around it. In large spaces we can establish different centers of attention with distinct furniture. However, this is something which should not be taken too far.

Tapestries and old paintings, antic window frames and doors, are other elements that should be considered as old furniture. Restoring or reforming them is another possibility for enriching the space. Good reforming or renovation always manages to introduce new features while conserving the old ones and leaving the building with its venerable character. Some furniture can seem rather dull unless it has a certain style, and it will have to be us who give it. A daring coat of paint, or stripping off the paint and revarnishing, can convert an apparently boring piece of furniture into the center of attention. Creativity is the key.

Some piece of antique furniture are especially decorative.

Worn wood on old furniture is noble and inviting.

Ambiences created with old furniture benefit from its integrity.

An old ceiling restored embellishes the space.

Restoring walls and ceilings

Restoring wal

Robust and attractive.

The walls and ceilings are the soul of the house, especially if it is old or has a country style. When we set about reforming a space like this, we must be open to the possibilities that we could discover. Underneath earlier reform work could be hidden the original walls of the building, more interesting than the idea we were planning. Any material found must be valued if it fits in with our necessities and if it is possible to bring it up to scratch. Stone walls or cob walls are attractive in their own right: the older they are, the more alluring, and where present will surely become one of the outstanding features of a space.

Ceilings offer us more or less the same opportunities. Probably the original, more interesting and attractive, ceiling is hidden behind a false one. Wooden beams, vaulted ceilings or even cornices and rosettes are worth restoring because they have enriching qualities, just as stone or brick walls do, giving texture and warmth to the space and increasing the value of the house.

If the building is not old enough to have a valuable structure, or if it is too far gone to be worth restoring, we must consider totally refurbishing the walls and ceilings. Although the practice of laying new coverings on top of old ones is common, it is not the best option. A new hard, quality covering is obtained by stripping down

Blue tones on the wall enhance the rural aspect.

Country design offers singularly attractive, traditional spaces.

the walls until you come to a solid, healthy structure, suitable for the application of a new covering.

Colors and textures

Sensitive and expressive. Colors fill our homes and our lives, influencing our perception of everything around us, and even our mood. Color, closely related to the illumination, is one of the key ingredients in the decoration. Applying paint and a brush is a way of radically changing the style and ambiance of a place without needing to modify either the architecture or the furniture.

Color is essential to the character of a space.

It is very difficult to determine which colors go together and which clash because everybody's perception is different. Classifying the colors is not practical because there is no universal guide to taste. What is more useful when choosing colors is to think about the characteristics of the space and what we are trying to confer on it.

The purity, cleanliness and luminosity of white means that it radiates peace and tranquillity. However, if we abuse it, we will make the spaces too cold and impersonal. Blue is the color of harmony and relaxation. It brings freshness and calm to the spaces it decorates, making them seem bigger than they actually are. Green reminds us of nature with all its stillness and grace and gives us a cozy feeling. Yellow is by definition a warm color

Blue makes the spaces more harmonious and relaxing.

Different tones of ceramics confer a rural look on the space.

Colors & textures

which breathes life and vigor into the spaces, encouraging us to be active surrounded by its luminosity. Red is powerful and energetic so it has to be used carefully, in moderation. Some of its shades are too bright, aggressive or even clashing. Neutral tones, like beige, cream colors or ivory have the advantage of never going out of fashion. They combine easily with whites and yellows so can resolve all sorts of decoration dilemmas.

Often we forget to get the most out of the textures. The modern trends in design, influenced by minimalism, have pushed them aside. Rustic, country styles are trying to recover elements from the past that used textures to enrich the space. Some examples of textures which are being lost are wall tapestries, embroidery on cushions and curtains, and velvets. Decoration has to reinforce anything that stimulates the senses. Old, worn wood, hand crafted ceramics or any object with a curious texture can be put to use to embellish the decoration.

The textures of the materials in a space are also decisive in determining its ambiance. Smooth surfaces like glass, marble or metal freshen up the space and give it vitality as they reflect back the light. However, they tend towards coldness. The rougher, more textured surfaces like wood, ceramic, or natural fiber are warmer and more relaxing.

Blue and white is a classic combination, always fresh and ageless.

Neutral and earth tones combine easily to give a joyful effect.

Warm & comfortable materials

Outdoor furniture

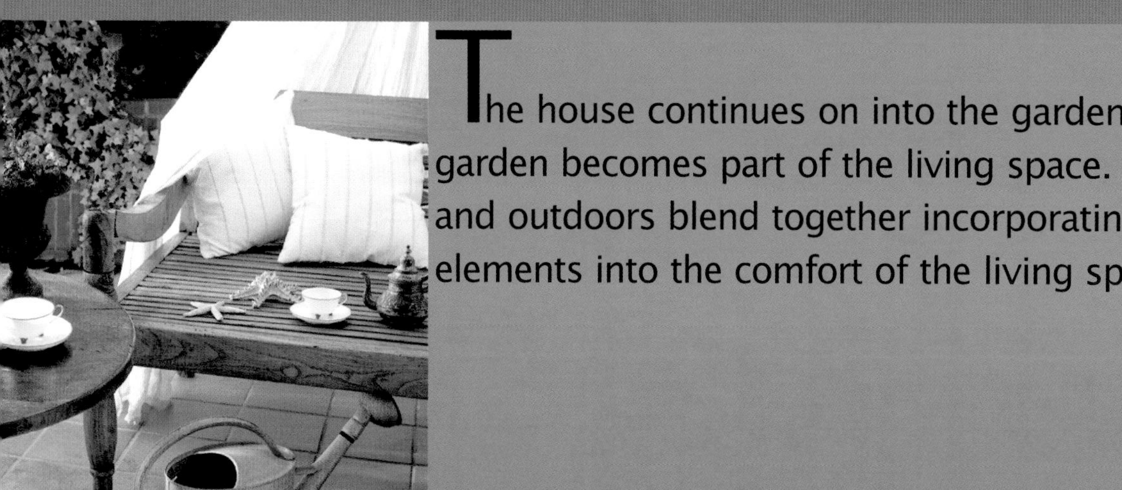

The house continues on into the garden and the garden becomes part of the living space. Indoors and outdoors blend together incorporating natural elements into the comfort of the living space.

Pools & terraces

Delightful relax

A time to rest

Warm and comfortable materials

Warm and natural.

The materials used in gardens and terraces have to respect the environment and adapt to form part of the natural scenery. The architecture of the house will lay down the style to be followed in the garden. A country house with natural materials and textures should have terraces, gardens and porches overflowing with vegetation, and the materials should be natural or hand-finished, like stone or terra-cotta. They give an uneven, rustic look which unobtrusively blends in with the greenery and flowers.

The furniture has to follow the same criteria. Some wicker or bamboo cane armchairs are light yet robust. They can subtly form part of the ambiance, not in the foreground, but quietly integrated into the overall effect.

Natural fabrics like cotton or linen give outdoors some of the qualities of indoors. Silk printed cloths can invigorate the spaces by introducing a dash of color among the greenery and natural materials.

Accessories are essential for giving character to these spaces. Lamps to light up the night, flower pots, rose beds and even ceramic or wood pieces are key elements to turn the garden or terrace into a decorative space.

The colors of the walls can be set off against the natural features and the tones of the flowers and plants. Green, yellow, pink and violet are lively, cheerful colors bequeathed to us by nature and brought into our home by flowers and plants.

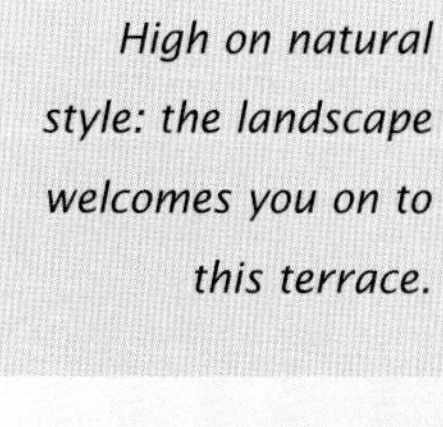

High on natural style: the landscape welcomes you on to this terrace.

Outdoor furniture

Sturdy and comfortable.

Furniture is normally associated with indoors but the comfort it offers can be taken to the garden or the terrace, enabling us to create an indoor ambiance outside, for example a dining room, a living room or even a kitchen. A table with some chairs around it can mark off a meeting area or gathering point. A few wood or iron benches or armchairs can create a little lounge beneath a porch or a canopy.

Too quiet to be true, only the gentle lapping of the pool can be heard.

Outdoor furniture

Get the world off your back: relax in this soft garden sofa.

Fabrics and cushions will make everything more comfortable and give a warm, protected indoor feeling in these spaces.

Natural and resistant materials like wood, iron, cane and even stone are the most suitable, both for practicality and for aesthetics. The climate, the rain, the sun, wind or snow can be abrasive so the furniture must be well conserved and protected.

A porch, a canopy, a sun screen or even trees and plants can help to establish a natural barrier between the different spaces. They are also useful for closing off a space, making it more cozy, or for sheltering the furniture from the weather. The swimming pool is another important gathering point. Around it we will layout deckchairs and other furniture so that we can enjoy relaxing moments of leisure by the pool.

The indoors and outdoors decoration must work together, complementing each other, if we want the effect to be unified and balanced. The furniture placed outside, seen through the windows, creates a close link with indoors. The sight of the plants and flowers brings nature into our home, while the garden is enhanced by its indoor qualities.

Delightful relaxation

Peaceful and magical. Gardens can be converted into magical, tranquil and mystical spaces, ideal for

Wicker furniture and treated wood give an informal character to this open air dining room.

Inside and outside come into contact. Nature is part of our lives.

winding down and forgetting the stress. Architecture comes into its own outside, matching itself against nature as it creates its own forms with its own materials, conceiving spaces which stand out from the surroundings. Human kind shows that they have power over nature and can control it. Plants, bushes, and trees grow in flower pots or beds, supervised by the gardener. The result is a space where you feel in contact with nature, but maintaining a certain distance. Order and rationality in the space enable us to create balanced, harmonious ambiance, optimal for relaxing and resting. The influence of oriental culture has brought into existence a type of garden different to the traditional European style due to the way the elements are rationalized. The space is organized aiming at order and equilibrium, toning down the wild aspects of nature. The materials, too, and the way they are worked on, are less natural. Finely polished stones placed at right angles or in perfect curves, or the straight lines of the swimming pool are elements that make us aware that there is a man-made tendency at work clearly different from the natural landscape. The outside area has similarities with the inside area.

The furniture, too, manifests this rationality. The decorative elements are reduced to the minimum: only what makes the garden more comfortable and cozy, like cushions or fabrics.

Water is the magical element that bestows mystery on these spaces. Tradition has always associated it with curing and its aesthetics are difficult to match for refinement and enchantment. The reflections on the surface, the ripples and its changing color give an ideal atmosphere for getting away from all the stress.

The external architecture limits the spaces as if it were a living room.

Water is like a blessing. The oriental influence is the final touch to this place for relaxation.

A pool in the country. Stone and water invite us to relax.

A time to rest

Relaxing and tranquil. Gardens are spaces for rest and relaxation, the perfect places for leisure and enjoying oneself because the contact with the open air helps us to wind down. Water plays a role with its special delight, difficult to find in other elements.

The swimming pool, especially in the Mediterranean gardens, is a key part both for its aesthetics and for its functionality. Whatever it is like, straight lined, curved, in green or blue tones, bordered by stone or wood, it confers character on the garden around it and reveals something about the personality of the residents.

If you want a minimalist and balanced space, the key lies in straight lines and austere forms and materials. Natural materials are the most suitable for this purpose. The zone around the pool is converted into a splendid lounge where deck chairs and sun-beds, or even a sofa, create a pleasant place for resting and meditating. There is no doubt that here too the oriental influence has made itself felt.

The surrounding flowers and greenery are an unmatchable source of inspiration and stimulation for our senses. The sweet fragrance of the petals or plants, the freshness of the wind, the bright colors that delight our eyes, all of these contribute to making these spaces unique.

Only the infinite sky is purer than the lines that define this space.